When he died in 1937 at age 92, his long life was the least of countless miracles attributed to Brother André of Montreal.

Today he is Blessed André, beatified in 1982 by Pope John Paul before a throng of pilgrims in St. Peter's Square. This acclaimed biography — assembled from the same documents and eyewitness testimony later used by the Vatican to examine his cause — was written when many of those who knew him were still alive. It is back in print after 40 years.

The venerated Brother who died in 1937 lives again in the pages of Mrs. Burton's absorbing narrative." — *The Sign*

"As a champion of devotion to Saint Joseph, and of his marvelous work in Montreal, there is a great deal to be said, and it is told graciously here." — *America*

Pope John Paul II prays at the tomb of Blessed André on September 11, 1984, during his visit to Canada.

$19.95

The portrait of Blessed André that was placed on the facade of St. Peter's Basilica during the beatification ceremony there on May 23, 1982.

BLESSED ANDRÉ
OF MOUNT ROYAL

By Katherine Burton

ROMAN CATHOLIC BOOKS
P.O. Box 2286
Ft. Collins, CO 80522-2286

Nihil obstat : REV. ARTHUR J. HOPE, C.S.C.
Imprimatur : ✠ MOST REV. JOHN F. NOLL, D.D.

August 1, 1952

This edition first published in 1952

ISBN 0-912141-38-7

The virtues and good works of
Brother André, visible in every one of
these pages, inspires this dedication

TO SAINT JOSEPH

Publisher's Note

Some significant dates since this book was first published:

• The basilica of St. Joseph's Oratory was completed in 1966.

• On June 12, 1978, Brother André was declared venerable by Pope Paul VI.

• On May 23, 1982, Pope John Paul II beatified Brother André in a ceremony in St. Peter's Square, attended by over 30,000.

• On September 11, 1984, Pope John Paul II prayed at the tomb of Blessed André during his visit to Canada.

The beatification ceremony in St. Peter's Square on May 23, 1982.

I AM pleased to have the opportunity of writing the foreword to this new edition of Katherine Burton's story of Brother André. It permits me to express for the Congregation of Holy Cross the gratitude to God and to St. Joseph which we all feel for the privileges given to us—Brother André our confrère, and the Oratory of St. Joseph our precious charge. The sources of this story, here so beautifully told, the documents, the accounts of witnesses and of grateful clients of St. Joseph, are now in the hands of Roman advocates who are examining them carefully for sufficient evidence of heroic virtue to warrant declaring the humble Brother blessed. We await submissively the decision of the Holy See.

It is now fifteen years since Brother André died. Each of those years has made us realise more fully his words : "When someone does something good on earth it is nothing compared to what he will be able to do once he gets to Heaven." His work goes on : the great basilica grows more complete, more beautiful ; the sick, the maimed, the sinners come and are comforted ; the love of St. Joseph spreads further over the world and deeper into the hearts of men. It is well for our time to have known this loving servant of St. Joseph, to see the power of God displayed through obedience, poverty, humility, and simple trust in Him. Our generation in its independence, its material wealth, its pride and scepticism, has been set upon and almost overwhelmed by the power of evil, and is nearly in despair before it. Brother André tells us : "With the help of God and of Mary, we shall surely conquer communism. The remedy is simple. More of us must pray. It will end when we pray more." This is the same message Mary

7

gave at Lourdes and at Fatima. Pray that all men hear and heed it. Pray, too, that God will honour His humble servant.

CHRISTOPHER J. O'TOOLE, C.S.C.,
Superior General
Congregation of Holy Cross.

Preface

THE life of Brother André, by Katherine Burton, was first published in *The Ave Maria*. Each week I was eager to read Mrs. Burton's pages. And I was not the only one. I know several who, conquered as they were by the author's forceful yet charming style and the interesting life story she was writing, felt a repeated urge as well as a persistent duty to pass the magazine on to friends.

Pliny the Younger is quoted as saying: "Happy are those gifted people able to write things fit to be read." Katherine Burton has this rare quality. From her pen have come several works which have been highly appreciated by a host of readers. Her life of Brother André will, I am sure, bring her even greater fame for she has put her whole soul into probing the depths of a character that will surely win the hearts of all upright men and women.

When Mrs. Burton decided to write the life of this humble Brother of Holy Cross, she immediately set out for St. Joseph's Oratory where she might breathe the very atmosphere in which her hero had sanctified himself. In and around the Shrine everything spoke of the past in answer to the many queries that had to be answered before sufficient information could be secured. Mrs. Burton left Montreal with the pertinent data she needed for her book. Unexpectedly, she left St. Joseph's Oratory quite another woman. Now she could read meaning into what heretofore she had been able only to surmise. With a wonderful sense of truth she visualizes the scenes of Alfred Bessette's boyhood days; she puts appropriate words on the lips of the boy's parents, relatives, and friends; she describes their attitudes and actions in so vivid a way that one might well think Brother

André himself whispered some of his secrets to her.

The subsequent years of the holy Religious have been described with sustained literary art. Throughout the book there is life, movement, exactness in minor details, there are smiles and tears ; there are the hopes and sorrows of St. Joseph's apostle ; there are Brother André's witty, good-natured retorts, so effective for filling hearts with optimism ; there are traits of human frailty and examples of Divine assistance.

Just as a distant mountain becomes more fascinating as one draws nearer to its magnificent garment of green, so does Brother André's definite character stand out more clearly as one fingers one's way to a full view of Brother's great spirit of faith, the basic principle on which he grounded his trust in God and in St. Joseph, his piety which ever remained as fresh and as perfumed as spring-tide, his humility which made him truly gracious towards all who came to him suffering in soul or in body, his heroic poverty, and even his slips of impatience which contributed to his genuine spirit of humility. Brother André, as described by Mrs. Burton, is a man who availed himself of all the means of personal sanctification until the last day of his life.

Brother André practised detachment in everything. He ate and slept because it was necessary to maintain his health. He asked for a new religious habit when the old one had turned green on his thin, bony shoulders. He travelled because his mission made it imperative that he, God's chosen one, should make St. Joseph known to the world. He bore without complaint his many infirmities. But one must have an ideal ; one cannot live devoid of all love. So Brother André was attached to God in proportion as he forsook the things of this earth. By meditating on St. Joseph, he grew in the love and service of the Divine Ideal with a simplicity so great that some of his confrères wondered why he deserved to be looked upon as a saint.

Katherine Burton has grasped this trait in the character of the apostle of Mount Royal. And for a very good reason. When she visited the Oratory, her first impression was, if not one of indifference, one of semi-deception. She wanted to contact the very soul of Brother André, but nothing at the Shrine seemed to reveal it to her. Then she entered the crypt, and saw Brother's simple tomb of plain black marble engraved with the words *Frère André*. She was overwhelmed. She saw poverty lurking even in the decay of the tomb and working to the greater glory of God and St. Joseph. Absolute detachment, then as now, is a constant reminder of Divine love, and death has not been able to stifle its voice.

Poor both in spirit and in action, with St. Joseph as his model, Brother André lived only for Christ and His most pure Mother. He never considered his devotion to the Patriarch of Nazareth as an end; it always remained a means to an end. From Joseph he learned how to love Mary, how best to honour and serve her at all times. He also learned to love and imitate Jesus. The Holy Eucharist was the great passion of his life. He was delighted to hear Mass, to serve the priest at the altar, to receive Holy Communion each morning, to pray in his obscure place behind the altar where he felt more at ease to attend the Holy Sacrifice, uniting himself all the more perfectly to the Divine Victim. His regular hour of adoration was for him a period of repose, though he made it late every night, after he had fulfilled all his duties, receiving the afflicted or visiting the sick. With what piety he made the Stations and meditated on the immolation of Jesus! Although he often recommended a novena to St. Joseph to his clients, he insisted still more often that they receive the Sacraments. He exhorted with such simplicity that those who sought his help felt they should do something about making their lives more holy.

I was only a boy when I first met Brother André. He was laying the foundation of the devotion to St. Joseph of Mount

Royal. I spent the first five years of my priesthood in his company, and later on, as Superior of St. Joseph's Oratory, I shared the roof that covered us both and concealed from profane eyes the hopes and sufferings of the holy Religious. I anointed Brother and was present when he died. I find him, as I knew him, in these sincere, living pages of Mrs. Burton.

✠ ALBERT F. COUSINEAU, C.S.C.
Coadjutor Bishop of Cap Haitien, Haiti.

CONTENTS

Page

CHAPTER ONE

ALFRED BESSETTE BECOMES BROTHER ANDRÉ

On a pleasant day in mid-August of 1845 a little procession walked slowly to the church in the village of Saint-Gregoire d'Iberville. Isaac Bessette came first, carrying his two-day-old son to the church for baptism. Edouard Bessette and Josephine Foisy, aunt and uncle of the baby and also his godparents, followed.

Josephine took a few hurried steps when they were near the church and caught up with the father. "Isaac, are you sure he is all right? He is so quiet."

She picked up the shawl that hid the baby from view and then fell back reassured. Her fear was a reasonable one, for the baby had been so frail and had so slight a hold on life when he was born that he had been baptized at the very moment of his birth. But now he had lived through a day and a night and was being brought to church for the ceremonies of baptism.

None of his three relatives could read or write so Père Sylvestre wrote in the parish register: "On August 10, 1845, we have baptised conditionally Alfred, born the previous day, of the lawful wedlock of Isaac Bessette, carpenter, and of Clothilde Foisy, of this parish," and he signed his own name in lieu of theirs.

They carried Alfred back to his home, where Madame Bessette took him in her arms, listened anxiously to his breathing, and then, giving him back to Josephine, sank weakly against her pillow. The older brothers and sisters clustered around to see the new baby, who slept soundly in the shelter of his aunt's devoted, supporting arms.

The house in which he was born was a rough structure, little more than a shack. It was some distance outside the town itself, in the midst of a half-cut forest from which the logs that made its walls had been hewn. But they were well fitted and the cracks between were packed with clay against the cold Canadian winter. There was hardly room enough though for the family of eight. They only light they had was from a single lamp, and the only decoration of any sort was a large crucifix which hung from a peg on the wall. Alfred and his brothers and sisters grew up, as they were born, under the badge of poverty.

The youngest baby in the family continued to be delicate, and perhaps it was due only to his mother's loving care that his life was saved. It was not much she could give him besides her love, for the father of the family earned only a bare living at his work of carpentering. The older children worked when they could find an odd job in the village and Madame Bessette kept house and cooked for the ever hungry brood.

There was little time for play in the household ; there were few playthings, save a few rude toys fashioned by their father. By the time Alfred was four years old, three more children had been added to the family, and Alfred, though still delicate and still his mother's especial care, was no longer treated as a baby but as a child who was old enough to perform small chores.

Since there was little chance to make a living for the family in Saint-Gregoire, Isaac Bessette determined to move to Farnham, a small town some distance away, where he was able to take up the trade of wheelwright and so make a slightly better living. There was enough bread now, even though there was often no butter to spread on it.

Here they followed the same pattern of hard work. The Bessettes followed also the routine which had been theirs ever since their marriage, for they were devoted to their Faith. In both the villages where they had lived they went to Mass on

Sundays, but the rest of their devotional life was carried out at their own fireside. Each morning they gathered their brood about them before the crucifix on the wall, and each evening they recited the rosary in unison.

There was deep love of God in the humble home. The children were taught that He made the birds and animals and made the wheat grow, that He was born in a crib as plain as theirs, and that He died on a cross for the Bessettes as well as for the rest of the world, that He loved children and they must love Him. Saint Joseph, the workman's model, was daily in Isaac Bessette's family prayers.

Alfred usually managed to be close to his mother and followed the prayers on her beads. She would give him a smile now and then or a loving look, as he knelt beside her and fingered the rosary she held, and she saw how the flickering firelight made rosy the little face that was really so pale. There was about this one child of hers something that in some way set him apart from the others—what she did not really know, but there was an awareness about him as he knelt there that was different. And she noticed how he touched the beads always with a sureness, an affection not common in so small a child.

Four years went by and during all those years Isaac Bessette worked hard to support his family. But poverty grew worse and more acute; and then one day came utter tragedy. "Isaac is hurt. A tree has fallen on him," a neighbour rushed in to tell Madame Bessette. When they brought her husband home, the hurriedly summoned doctor could only shake his head and order them to send for the priest; there was nothing he could do for the broken body. And a day later Isaac Bessette was laid to rest in the village cemetery.

Clothilde Bessette faced squarely her problem of providing alone for her brood. The neighbours did their best to help with food and by taking one or other of the children into their homes for a while. But the chief burden fell on the mother. After four years of working day and night, she fell a victim to tuberculosis.

Her relatives joined forces to help her and to take charge of the children. She herself went to stay with her sister Madame Timothé Nadeau, taking Alfred with her. He had always been her favourite, though she dearly loved all her children. But her reasonable excuse for keeping him with her instead of one of the others was his continued frailty. Besides, he had always been the one who could console and comfort her most, and she needed such consolation now, for she knew she had only a short time left to live.

She worried at times because Alfred was getting so little schooling. It was not that he lacked the chance, but he was never well enough to go for more than a week or so at a time. Due no doubt partly to the poverty of his first years, which necessitated insufficient food, the little strength he was born with had become even less, and a happy week of school would end in a period of semi-illness.

There was no one in the house who could teach him. His aunt was too busy with her own work and her own family, in addition to the care of her sister who was getting weaker daily and required more nursing ; and his uncle laboured all day on the rough acres of his farm, so could not give the boy more than a kindly passing attention.

Alfred was twelve years old when his aunt came to call him early one morning. "Alfred, your mother is dying. We have sent for your brothers and sisters. She has asked to see all of you together once more."

With the others Alfred went into her room and made one of the group around her bed. Some of them he had not seen for a long time and they were, to his childish gaze, grown up people now. Madame Bessette looked at them all in turn. Her voice was weak but very clear as she gave them her last wishes.

"Pray for me," she told them. "Don't forget your father's grave. I want to be buried in the cemetery beside him." She would have said more, but Madame Nadeau stopped her. "You must not exert yourself any more, Clothilde." So Madame Bessette gave a last smile to her family as they began to file from the room in response to their aunt's gesture. "I shall watch over you from heaven," she called after them.

Alfred's life was shattered anew. This time the blow was harder than the others had been. Often his mother had talked with him of the day when the family would all be happily united again, and now that hope was broken forever. His one consolation was remembering that his mother had asked them to pray for her. That he could do, and often when everyone was asleep Alfred would still be on his knees offering up Pater Nosters and Aves for his mother's soul. And one other consolation he had : the promise she had given her children that she would watch over them from heaven.

He needed consolation, for his uncle, a strong rugged man himself, began to insist that the boy do work of some kind as all of his own children were doing.

"You are more than twelve years old, Alfred," he told the boy. "I was out ploughing fields when I was that old. You will have to help earn your own living now, for you know we are not rich people and your health doesn't seem good enough to keep you in school nor do you show much ability when you do go. Perhaps some light work is the answer."

Alfred nodded soberly, but his uncle looked at him with some misgivings. Certainly this frail lad would never make much of a farmer. The shoemaker in the village needed an apprentice, he had heard, so he had the boy apprenticed there, and all day long Alfred bent absorbedly over the thick hides in the shop. He wanted very much to make his uncle proud of him, and his mother too, for he knew she was watching over his efforts. The awl was hard to master and pricked him often ; and at first the hammer gave him some hard blows on his fingers. But he was beginning to master the trade and felt happy that now he would soon be doing his part in his uncle's house.

His aunt, who had been watching him closely, spoke to her husband about the boy's health, after Alfred had been with the shoemaker for some months. The disease which had carried off his mother would, she was afraid, soon attack Alfred too if he did not have work that gave him fresh air instead of keeping him pent in an airless shop the whole day. So he was re-apprenticed, to the village baker this time ; but before long that too proved too heavy work for him, so his Uncle Timothé decided to let him help on the farm instead.

During the year after his mother's death Alfred made his First Holy Communion in the village church at Saint-Césaire. Father Provençal had prepared the boy carefully ; and he knew his catechism well and was familiar, from hearing them told over and over, with the stories of the Gospels. And the curé stimulated too the affection Alfred had felt even as a little boy for Saint Joseph—the great obscure, the curé called him. "Pauper, servus et humilis," he had said of him one day ; and then he explained the meaning of the Latin words to the catechism class.

His mother had laid well the loving foundation for his religious faith. Through her he had learned about Jesus, who loved children ; and she taught her own brood that it was their duty to love Him in turn. And Saint Joseph had been often in her prayers.

Now Alfred learned more about the great patriarch from Father Provençal who had an especial devotion to the saint and called him the model of workers. He managed to say something about him in every catechism class which Alfred attended. He also told them how old a friend of Canada Saint Joseph was, and how, as far back as 1624, when Quebec was only a little military trading post, the Recollect Fathers had placed their apostolic labours there under his protection and proclaimed him first patron of the land.

In this class Alfred mingled for almost the first time of his life with boys of his own age. After Mass he and the others used to stand around and listen to their elders discuss the affairs of the village and the country. Most of them worked so hard during the week that this was for them the one hour when they could exchange opinions or hear the events of the week told.

Alfred used to shiver in his shabby overcoat and muffler as he watched the sturdy crowd, and men in rough homespun, their collars high about their ears, their coats and caps lined with fur pelts they had themselves trapped. The women's clothes were as plain as their husbands', and most of them wore shawls instead of hats. Occasionally there would be a coat of rare pelts and a brightly coloured scarf, but these were few. The children looked much like their elders, for most of them wore clothes cut down from discards of their parents or from suits which their elder brothers or sisters had outgrown.

On the day of his First Holy Communion Alfred's uncle had his picture taken, and his aunt put it on the chest along with those of his cousins. It showed a pale face, hair carefully brushed, serious eyes, a pointed chin over a white tie. In one hand he held the ornate little prayer book which had been his aunt's gift to him.

One Sunday after Mass there was a stir of excitement in a group gathered about Father Provençal. He was talking to a tall young man whose clothes looked different from those of the village people.

"Who is he?" whispered Alfred to the nearest boy.

"It's Pierre ———. He used to live here but he went away before you came. He's been in the United States."

Alfred looked at the stranger with admiration. He had heard of the United States of course, but this was the first time he had ever seen anyone who had actually been in that fabulous land.

"You find it a good place to work?" asked Father Provençal.

The young man nodded vigorously. "Wonderful! You make money—more money than you can imagine here. The cities need men and they pay well and you don't have to worry about the pennies the way you do here. And you don't have weather like this either," he added, putting his handsome cap closer around his ears.

"Don't they have snow there?" asked an astonished voice.

"Of, of course!" There was condescension in his voice. "But not driving blizzards like ours. Snow, of course, but you don't have to be afraid when you get on the other side of the big river that you will freeze to death."

"Are you going back?"

He laughed again. "Am I going back? Just as soon as I have had a good visit with my folks. When I get as much in a week as I could make in a month around here—why wouldn't I go back?"

Father Provençal's quiet voice was heard again. "And you find a church for Mass on Sundays too?"

"Oh, yes, Father. Very near the big factory where I work there is a Catholic church and the priest can speak French too, and so do many of the people around there," he said proudly.

Alfred went home with dreams in his eyes and in his heart the determination to get strong and well and some day go to the United States, too.

Meantime, with his uncle's willing permission, he began hiring himself out to the farmers around Saint-Césaire. He would work as an extra labourer for one or other of the farms in the neighbourhood. They gave him the lighter tasks to do, leaving the harder work for the husky labourers whom Alfred never ceased to envy for their prowess at lifting and sawing.

Suddenly this work was interrupted in turn, but this time not because of ill health. Timothé Nadeau decided to join the gold rush to California, along with hundreds of other Canadians who saw a chance to make there the money they had never been able to draw from their farms. Before he left he settled all the family, Alfred with them, at Farnham, near Quebec.

The boy found work as a farm labourer on the farm of Mr. Ouimet on the outskirts of the village, work that was not too hard for him. And he found a friend in the person of Father Springer, curé of the village church. The timid lad who made his Communions with such eager zeal, who prayed so often and so long in the shadows of the church, attracted the curé's attention. He asked him one day to call at the rectory. When he came, he drew the shy youth to talking of the village and his work there, and finally of his own problems.

Alfred, who had found no confidant among his aunt's brood of teasing cousins, suddenly began to talk eagerly to this quiet, interested man. "I'm not strong," he stammered. "I want to work and then I can't. I am not lazy. But the farmers say I don't do enough to earn my meals. At home they knew me and gave me tasks not beyond my strength. Mr. Ouimet knows I am trying but I am afraid I don't do enough to pay my way. I wish—I want to work—I do really."

The priest looked at him thoughtfully. There was no use in telling this boy to go and join in the village games and mix with the youth of his own age. His health would scarcely warrant it, not after a hard day in the fields. But he felt something else about the lad too—a certain remoteness, a stillness as if Alfred were waiting for something, as if somewhere there was the sort of work he could do.

As Alfred looked about the room his eyes lighted on a picture of St. Joseph on the wall. It was ordinary enough, showing him at work in the carpenter's shop, Mary busy with her needle close by and the Child watching His father and leaning on one end of the bench. Alfred looked at the curé. "My father was a carpenter too," he said.

"A good trade—from Nazareth to now. You love St. Joseph, then, Alfred?"

He nodded soberly. "Oh, yes. At Saint-Césaire I used to pray to him often and ask him to give me a job I could really be worthwhile at doing. But so far he has not found it for me," he added sadly.

The curé stood up and patted the boy's shoulder. "He will. Wait and see. Some day he will find the exact task you are fitted for and you will be strong enough to do it."

More and more conversations followed this first one. Alfred told him about his mother and how he had loved her and she him. "You see, I was a sickly child and so she fussed with me more than the others. Sometimes she gave me little dainties that must have meant great denial to her. I always was the one who knelt beside her and followed the rosary on her beads. She had the loveliest smile, Father. I see her often and she smiles at me and gives me looks of love. She doesn't speak to me but she doesn't need to. Her love shines on me warmer than words."

"You keep her in your prayers often, I know," said the curé with sympathy.

One day Mr. Ouimet came home from an auction sale, and at the supper table he showed the family some of the things he had bought. Among them was a crucifix and he noticed his farm hand looking at it with longing eyes. "Would you like this for your own, Alfred?" he asked him.

"Oh, yes, sir, very much."

When he had received it Alfred took it to the barn with him, shining it on his sleeve as he went. Later in the evening, Mr. Ouimet, wondering why his farm hand stayed so late in the barn, went out to see what was keeping him up. In a corner he saw the crucifix shining in the light of the lantern set on the shelf. On his knees before it, so absorbed he had not heard Mr. Ouimet's step, was Alfred still as a statue.

His employer was not an emotional man, but his commonplace barn seemed to him full of something more than its daylight commonplaceness. It was like the setting in the church at Christmas time in a way—the straw on the floor, the cows looking over their boarded enclosures, the still figure in the dim light, like a shepherd come to worship.

Alfred told the curé about his new place for prayer, which Father Springer thought excellent and gave him a little figure of St. Joseph to put there. Alfred's fervency in prayer seemed to him a thing that should be cultivated and he meant to see more of the boy and gain more of his confidence.

But there was something which Alfred had not mentioned to the curé. He had gone to stay with his aunt for a few days because one of his fits of illness was on him. She helped him into bed and noticed that he drew in his breath in uncontrollable pain when she touched him. Then she felt something hard under his shirt.

"What is that thing under your clothes?" she demanded.

He pushed away from her touch. "Nothing, aunt, really nothing."

"Let me see it, Alfred." Opening his shirt, she saw an iron chain close about the boy's thin waist.

"Alfred," she said reproachfully, "You shouldn't do that. Promise me you won't wear that thing again."

He promised, for it was like promising his mother. But the next day one of his cousins said at table, "Look, Alfred, aren't our beds good enough for you anymore? He's sleeping on the floor, mother—what do you think of that?"

She shook her head worriedly. "Alfred, you must get well and strong or you will never get any real work done in the world."

Father Springer had been watching his protege's health too, and between them, he and Mr. Ouimet decided the work on the farm was beyond the lad's strength. Father Springer offered instead to make him his chore boy and let him live in the rectory.

Alfred took with him only his crucifix and his statue of St. Joseph and his few worn garments. He was happy in this new work. Now he did not have to build his own prayer corner. He had a whole church to go into for his prayers, where St. Joseph stood tall on one side of the altar and Our Lady was at the other, and between them, in a simple tabernacle, was their Son.

He was in good hands now. The kindly curé saw that he did not over-exert and so, husbanding his strength, Alfred became unusually well. He was very happy for almost the first time since his mother's death. Often in the darkness he saw her gentle smile and knew she was happy to know that he was, and all day as he worked he felt her love hover over him. And St. Joseph too, whom, next to Jesus and His Mother, Alfred loved most of heaven's host, was watching over him.

*   *   *

When Alfred Bessette was twenty years old he was growing more and more restless. It was not that he did not like his work nor that he felt any less of an affection for Father Springer ; but so many of the young men of the village had gone away to work and come home again for a visit with stories of the great opportunities in the United States that Alfred felt an increasing desire to go to this land of opportunity.

Father Springer agreed that it might be a good idea. He would be happy to keep Alfred with him indefinitely, but he knew that was no future for a young man with ambition ; and Alfred, though no taller than the average lad of fifteen, was really a grown man. His face was thin and pale as ever, and he was far from being a stalwart person, but he was much stronger than he had been, thanks no doubt to the good care the curé had given him.

"Besides there are not the severe winters we have here," said Father Springer. "But could you be sure of a position when you get there?"

That, Alfred told him, would be taken care of. Father would remember the Pierre who sometimes came to see friends in the village—had been in the United States for some years and would be going back again soon. He had promised to find employment for Alfred and to send for him as soon as he found a likely job.

A month went by with no word. Then one day Alfred came in great excitement, a letter in his hand. "Here, Father, it is from the United States. Will you read it to me?"

The curé sighed. If only the lad could read, then he could have done so much more for him. But with no education, of what use was it? He opened the letter and told the eager Alfred that Pierre had found work for him at a cotton mill near Plainfield in the state of Connecticut.

Alfred made his simple preparations, said good-bye to his aunt and those of his brothers and sisters who were near enough, and to his cousins and the people he knew in the village, and to the curé. Last of all he said good-bye to Saint Joseph in the little church.

The night before he left he had a dream so vivid he thought he must have been awake and not asleep. He was working in a field in his dream, and he leaned for a moment on his rake to rest. He looked up to see Saint Joseph watching him with a tender look in his eyes and a smile on his face as loving as his own mother's smile. Alfred smiled back ; and then, feeling so tired he thought he could never begin working again, he asked a question of the kind old man looking at him.

"Where am I going to die, Saint Joseph?"

The patriarch seemed to melt away from before his eyes and in his place he saw a mighty stone building with towers and tall steps and a great cross on its summit. For a few moments it stood clear and white before him at the end of the field. Then it slowly dissolved and Alfred found himself sitting up in bed. It was morning and time to open the church for Mass.

He told the curé about his dream later in the morning, and the curé smiled at the thought of his chore boy living, or dying either, in a great stone building. "But you are going to the United States. Who knows what may befall you there, Alfred?" he said, half in jest, half in earnest.

Alfred Bessette went to the United States with high hopes for his future. But the three years he spent in that country brought him nothing he had hoped for. And the reason was the same that had wrecked his other attempts—his wretched health. He liked the work at the mill at first, but soon the continued confinement within walls and in close air proved bad for a young man who had been most of his life outdoors. He had to give up finally with great regret the work Pierre had procured for him.

With no means of support, he did the obvious thing : went to seek employment on a farm as handy man. But work was scarce and there were many much stronger and more able than he eager to snatch the jobs. He wished with all his heart for better health so he might stay in the United States. He was beginning to love New England dearly. Despite its cold it was so much gentler than the harsh climate of his own land, and

there were many who spoke his own language—French
Canadians intent on making their way in the new country as
he wanted to do. The three years he spent there were by no
means wasted, but it became clearer and clearer to him that
he must find something else to do, must go somewhere else.

During these years he had written several times, aided by
friends who could write the letters for him, to his old friend
in Saint-Césaire—Father Provençal. And his friends read the
priest's letters to Alfred too. He had told of his almost hopeless
attempt to establish himself in the United States and in his last
letter he had rather hesitatingly mentioned his intention of
perhaps returning to Canada again. Now Father Provençal
wrote urging him strongly to return and added that he felt sure
there would be a place for him somewhere even if not on the
land or in a mill.

Alfred Bessette was twenty-three years old when he finally
decided to give up the tasks that were proving too much for
him and return to Canada. He went to stay at first with some
relatives at Sutton, a town quite near the border. Then he
journeyed on to see Father Provençal to discuss his future with
him. They sat together in the rectory, the tall old man and the
frail young one, and they talked of the uncertain future of the
latter. But this time Alfred revealed the dream that had long
been with him, and which he had always felt too humble, too
poor to mention aloud.

"Father," he asked, "don't you think I could enter the
religious life in some way? I have wanted to ever since I first
served your Mass here as a little boy ; and at Farnham I wanted
to, and when I went to Mass in the United States I felt the
desire and I still have it in me."

Father Provençal looked perplexed. The young man before
him was earnest and good, but more than that was needed to
determine a religious vocation. He had so little learning, he was

so sickly—how could he be ambitious to live a religious life even though he loved God with all his heart and wished to make every effort to serve Him?

"But, Alfred, what do you think you could do in such a life?" he asked.

Alfred shook his head. He did not know. "I love prayer— and silence—that I know. I hate this feverish vagabond's existence of mine. But I don't know what I can do." He looked suddenly up into Father Provençal's troubled face. "But one thing I am sure of, Father. I want in some way to spread devotion to Saint Joseph."

He looked at the curé almost pleadingly. "And often the thought has come to me that Saint Joseph wants me to do it," he said hesitantly. "In the United States I used to feel that, when I was in church, out of somewhere the thought would come to me again and again—I must do something for Saint Joseph."

The priest had been on the point of telling Alfred that he ought to find some other work, because a man who could not read or write and who had not even the rudiments of education would be out of place in the religious life. But this devotion to the Patriarch, which was so strong in the young man that it caused him to sit more erect when he spoke of it and made his eyes glow and gave his cheeks a sudden flush as if of health, finally made Father Provençal decide to think things over before he spoke in the negative as he had intended doing.

Surely, he mused, there must be a place for this lad in religion. And by evening it had come to him where the place was. Father Provençal had always a great interest in the education of the young, so much so that some years before he had raised funds to build a commercial college, the direction of which he had given over to the Congregation of Holy Cross. When Alfred first came to see him, the school was in its second year and flourishing, with six Brothers living and teaching in the fine new building opposite the location of the rectory.

When Alfred returned to learn the decision of the curé, Father Provençal asked him if he had ever thought of becoming a working Brother in some religious house.

His eyes shone. "But Father, you know I can't read or write. They will not let me enter, I am afraid," he said sadly.

"Well, that might not matter. After all, not all religious are teachers. That was the thought that came to me after you had gone. You see in a congregation, like the one there," and he nodded in the direction of the school, "there are Brothers who devote themselves to manual labour. Just as Saint Joseph lived and protected Our Lord in his hard task, so the Holy Cross Brothers aid the priest in his work of saving souls. How would you like to become a religious of Holy Cross?"

Alfred's eyes glowed. "Oh, Father, do you think perhaps I have a vocation? I had never even dared to hope for such a thing, when I know how ill-fitted I am."

Father Provençal made up his mind. "I am convinced of it, my son. Now go to the chapel and pray to God that He may enlighten you as to His wishes."

Alfred looked at him solemnly. "I will. And I will keep on and on praying until I know. And many thanks for helping me, Father."

Alfred was staying at the rectory for a while anyway, so it was easy to go often to the Church. The idea had been that he could help around the house as well as with the Masses. Later Father Provençal used to chuckle about that help around the house. "Whenever I needed his services, I found he was already busy—at the feet of Saint Joseph in my church."

Father Provençal told the Brothers in the school about the young man and his ambitions and his handicaps. He spoke frankly of his lack of education. If the young man could only read and write he could study at home until he was ready for high school or college, but this handicap of illiteracy seemed too great. Yet he felt the youth had a vocation and he asked them to grant the boy a personal interview.

The Brothers, deep in their work of organizing the school, were reluctant to talk to him at all, and so give him hope of joining them. An education was necessary to become a part of a teaching Order like theirs. But Father Provençal, more and more convinced of a vocation, urged them to give him at least an interview. Finally the Brothers consented, but obviously only to please the priest.

Alfred had spent the previous day almost entirely in prayer, especially in prayers to his chosen saint. He was still praying when he went to keep his appointment. He was ushered into the presence of two Brothers, who received him very kindly and made him feel at ease. The three sat in the plain little parlour of the backwoods rectory and talked together. The Brothers were already feeling for some way to dissuade the young man, to tell him as pleasantly as possible that he was ill-fitted for such work.

"Tell me," said one of them finally, "just why do you want to enter our community? Do you really feel you have a vocation?"

He looked at the Brother with glowing eyes. "I can't do any teaching and maybe I will never learn to read or write. But I can work. I will be glad to do any task no matter what it is if I am admitted. And besides I love Saint Joseph so much that I feel, if I were in his service, my health would grow better and I could do more and better work right along."

The two Brothers were amazed to see the quiet youth sit up very erect, to see his mild eyes grow bright and keen when he mentioned his patron and theirs. "I think Saint Joseph wants me to work for him," he told them simply but firmly.

At last the two visitors, almost against their better judgment, promised they would consult with their superiors and would recommend him to them as a postulant for the Congregation.

Alfred went back to his relatives at Sutton to wait for an answer, delighted at the possible chance of such a future. Perhaps this was what he had always wanted without being able to formulate the idea, without in fact daring to formulate it. He had brought his prayers to the feet of Saint Joseph, had begged him to find something to do that would aid his beloved saint; and now perhaps in addition to prayers he could give him the work of his hands. He could scrub for him and sweep for him—anything at all, so long as it helped Saint Joseph in his work of spreading the gospel of his dearly loved foster Son.

The two Brothers sent their recommendation to Father Julien Gastineau, at Montreal, who held the two offices of president of the college and master of novices. A letter from the curé at Saint-Césaire had also come to him, which opened in a rather startling way. "I am sending you a saint for your Congregation," wrote Father Provençal. He went on to say that he was aware of the young man's lack of learning, but he felt his zeal would be valuable in a congregation like Holy Cross. He had known the boy from childhood, he said, and could vouch for the good mind behind the unschooled brain. The love of God so filled the youth's heart that Father Provençal doubted there was room for anything else. He felt sure there was a place for Alfred since the members of the Congregation had as one of their objectives to produce in their lives the supernatural union of affection which existed between Our Lord and Saint Joseph.

When the curé had word that Alfred would be received as a postulant, his joy knew no bounds. He sent for Alfred and gave him much advice before the young man left for his new life: "Alfred, remember being a Brother is in every sense of the word being a religious. A Brother gives up possible honours and advantages. His is a complete sacrifice."

Alfred nodded solemnly and was silent, too moved to speak. The curé smiled suddenly. "Alfred, here is a thought to carry with you. Our Saviour was the first religious. He lived poor, chaste and obedient, because this was the divine way to show life to the world. That is how saints are made."

It was Alfred's turn to smile. "Well, that is one thing I needn't worry about—being a saint."

The curé smiled back and then was serious again. "After all, Alfred, saints are merely human beings. They become saints because they no longer exist—God lives in them."

With such recommendations to herald him, in the autumn of 1870 Alfred Bessette, now twenty-five years old, came to Montreal and went directly to the building which housed the novices of Holy Cross. He came during a famous year, for that winter Pope Pius IX proclaimed Saint Joseph patron of the Universal Church.

The land of Alfred's birth and especially the city to which he had come had always cherished Saint Joseph. Even in 1643 the devotion to Saint Joseph was so strong that his feast day was honoured with the firing of artillery guns ; and the first Indian baptized there had received the name Joseph. Montreal, the city of Mary, had always had a great affection for Mary's spouse. And the Congregation of Holy Cross came from France filled with fervour for him. Now here was one more of his clients come to work for him.

Alfred came to the long building on the western slope of Mount Royal, known as Bellevue hotel, which the Congregation had only the year before made into a combined college and novitiate transferring the former novitiate from Saint Laurent College to the house at Côte-des-Neiges.

The postulant examined his surroundings as he waited for the door to open. To his country eyes the grey building was an elegant affair. He looked across the street, to see only a mountain wild with undergrowth and interlacing trees. Then a black-robed Brother opened the door and the future miracle worker went out of the world he had always known into a new and very different one.

It was not always easy for even a yielding person like Alfred to meet all the demands of religious discipline after ten years in the world in a pattern of freedom. But Alfred had a purpose to love God and to serve Saint Joseph. For that even a high-spirited eager youth could give up his own desires completely. And the vocation of a Brother in religion was a life hidden in God with Christ—and that was what he yearned for.

The novice master found he had a docile subject. The spartan simplicity of the establishment was nothing new to Alfred who had always known poverty. Essentially of a happy disposition, he was pleased to see all these religious men about him not in gloomy silence but happy and joyous in their work. He laboured very hard during his first months to prove his worth. He washed dishes and waited at table, scrubbed floors and kept the corridors neat. He learned to help with the mending, especially the rough mending of the clothes of the field workers of the Community.

Two days after Christmas of that year, following a retreat, he was given the religious habit in the college chapel. Breathless with joy, he knelt while the habit was handed to him and heard the priest who presided say, "Alfred Bessette, henceforth thy name will be Brother André."

He liked the name immensely. Father Provençal's Christian name was André, and Father Provençal was his friend and adviser. Through days of routine in which work shared time with prayer young Brother André built up his spiritual life, making it conform to the best of his ability to the ideal of the divine pattern. Between hard work and hard praying he found his days well filled. Sometimes he thought it all really a joke of the good God—to fetch him, without a sou, with no learning, no health, to be His religious. But he was happy beyond words that it was so.

CHAPTER TWO

THE PORTER OF SAINT LAURENT

IN the year after Alfred Bessette came to Holy Cross, the religious at Saint Laurent College found they were too few in number to meet the increasing demands of the institution and asked for some of the novices to help them. A group was brought to live in the "white house," an old building with whitewashed walls, situated back of the college itself. The new novice was among them.

Here Brother André was made linen keeper and infirmarian and it was his task to keep the corridors spotlessly clean. He had a new spiritual director, Father Hupier, whom he as well as most of Montreal held in the highest esteem.

Life seemed to be in a settled groove at last for Alfred Bessette, now Brother André of Holy Cross. Then suddenly trouble threatened. He learned that his superiors were greatly concerned about his health, which had not improved very much. Although they liked him, they felt he could be of little use to the community if he were to become an invalid who would have to be taken care of instead of caring for others.

The novice was heartbroken. This was his life, his love, the place where he belonged the rest of his days. He knew he would always be well enough to be of use, but how could he convince the superiors of that? While he was waiting to hear the final decision in his case, Bishop Bourget one day came to visit the religious at the college. Brother André made up his mind to do a daring thing. He crept as quietly as he could down the hall to the bishop's door and gave a desperate knock.

"Come in," he heard before he could make up his mind to

37

turn and run. He mastered his fear and went in. The bishop
was sitting by the window in a tall chair : an old man with
snow-white hair and thin, worn features. He was seventy-two
years old, but he sat as erect as a man half his age. Seeing the
novice who clung to the door knob and dared not venture
closer, he said encouragingly, "What can I do for you, my
son?"

At the kindness in the voice Brother André crossed the room
with a rush. He held his hands closely together and fell on his
knees. "I am afraid I cannot become a religious," he faltered.
"They fear I have not the health for the work. But I have,
your excellency, and I have so great a love of God that I know
I will find the strength for any task they give me. It is my
life . . . must I leave here?"

The bishop put his hand on the bent head, and sat for a few
moments very still. Then he leaned over and patted the tightly
clasped hands. "Do not be afraid, my dear son. You will be
allowed to make your religious profession."

Brother André with that promise ringing in his ears, rose to
go. When he reached the door the bishop called to him. "Who
is your patron saint, Brother?"

"Saint Joseph, your excellency." The bishop smiled. "I love
him too," he said. "We will both pray that he may be honoured
here and soon, now that the Holy Father has declared him
Patron of the Universal Church."

He watched the young man go and remained in thought for
a few moments. Then he picked up a paper in which he had
written something on this very subject of which he had just
spoken to the wistful, pleading young man. He read the words
over : "We must have a church specially dedicated to his cult
in which he may receive daily the public homage worthy of
his eminent virtues. We wish to consecrate all our strength and
the rest of our life in making him honoured in such a church,

establishing there a place of pilgrimage where the people will come to him."

Still a little fearful of his daring, Brother André was greatly relieved when the master of novices whispered in his ear two days later, "Don't be worried or afraid. I shall see to it that you are admitted to your vows."

The master of novices felt it was a bit rash perhaps, but after all the bishop had urged it and he said to himself, "Well, if the young man becomes unable to work, he can at least pray for us." For he had watched him at his prayers and had been impressed by his devotion.

Brother André made his temporary vows with a happiness almost too great to bear. At the Community Mass he read the prescribed form in the presence of the priest. He had written it himself in his unskilled hand, for the Brothers were teaching him to read and to write a little. But he really learned it all by heart, though he followed the words with his eyes. "I, Joseph Alfred Bessette, Brother André, unworthy though I am, relying nevertheless on the divine mercy and earnestly desiring to devote myself to the service of the adorable Trinity, make to Almighty God the vows of poverty, chastity and obedience, promising to accept whatever employments it may please my superiors to entrust to me."

Later he wrote his Uncle Timothé, now back from the gold fields and living again with his family at Saint-Césaire. It was a joyous letter : "I am very happy in the state I have entered. The happiness which one knows in the house of God is so great that one finds continually new favours—favours which we place above all the pleasures of the world. We have not too much time to pray to God to grant us graces and to thank Him and to devote ourselves to our occupations. If you come to see me, it will be I who will open the door to you and we will take time for a talk together."

For a year Brother André went on with his duties of dishwasher and general handy man. Happy in his new position in life, his health improved so much that by the time he was ready, in 1872, to make his final vows, his superiors had decided he would make a desirable member of the community. He had a true vocation.

He was given his first assignment at the College of Notre Dame at Côte-des-Neiges as porter and general messenger, a post which happened to be vacant at the time, and for which post Brother André, who could not teach, seemed exactly the person. He was to answer the door-bell, find out the visitors' mission, and call the persons desired—not a very important job to the outer eye, but to Brother André it was work for God.

He had a little cell near the parlour which was his own, a small room not quite six feet square, where one window gave a dim light. There was a wardrobe, and a small desk and a bench along the wall. A couch with a thin mattress was pushed in one corner and on the walls were a crucifix and a picture of Saint Joseph. For Brother André the last two objects would have furnished any room ; for he could always sleep on the floor if he had to—in fact he often did, rolled in a coverlet. But he needed but little time for sleep when there were so many prayers to be said.

Before long he was given additional duties. There were not many religious in the house and they all worked very hard. The Brothers who taught were very busy with their classes for the school was growing constantly. They took boys from seven to twelve years of age, years which called for special care, and there were over two hundred of them to train and teach. So Brother André was appointed to awaken the religious at five in the morning, knocking at every door and saying, "*Benedicamus Domino.*" He rang the bell for the various school hours, besides keeping the parlour and corridors neat and orderly. He went to town for the mail, and ran errands there outside mail hours. On Mondays and Saturdays he took the students' laundry to the city to be sent home. Evenings he prepared the altar breads and made cinctures for the religious. And it was he who saw to it that Saint Joseph in the chapel always had fresh flowers before him.

One day he heard the superior express a wish for a lawn in front of the college. Brother André decided that was his job, too. He carried earth every evening and during spare moments of the day. For this task he pampered himself to this extent. He used two wheelbarrows in this pattern : he would push one for some distance and then go back and push the other a like distance. He wasted no time doing that, he assured himself, for he could say his rosary while walking back empty-handed to the alternate barrow.

The trouble with this last task was that he would at times find himself still working when he heard the crowing of the cock or when it was time to ring the bell to rouse the Community. Brother André did not need much sleep, just as he needed little food. He usually took a piece of bread, dipped it in milk and water, and called that his meal. He sat in one corner of a table in the refectory and took his meal in a hurry, for as porter he had to eat when he had the chance.

He took one more task on himself. At first he had cut the hair of one or two of the boys who were in a hurry and had no time to be taken to the village to have it done. Before long he was considered the school barber, so good was the technique he developed. He charged five cents for each haircut and put the small fees away carefully, intending to use the amount some day to further devotion to Saint Joseph. When that day came he would ask for permission to use it.

His own devotion to Saint Joseph had of course become general knowledge to the whole school, for at some time all religious and students had heard about the power of the great patron and the efficacy of prayers to him for the granting of favours.

Every moment that was not taken up by work Brother André gave to prayer. His morning Mass and daily Communion were followed by at least a half-hour of prayer. When he was helping about the sanctuary he made a deep genuflection always, even if he passed the tabernacle thirty times while arranging the altar. Sometimes one of the Brothers would take his place at the door, when Brother André earnestly begged him to so he might make an hour of adoration.

One unsuspecting Brother, newly come and not yet used to the porter's ways, did not warn him, as the other Brothers did, not to stay too long. He waited and answered the calls for visitors and then began to wonder just when Brother André was coming back. Finally, he went to the door of the chapel and found him intent on his knees before the altar. "But, Brother," he whispered, "you have been two hours praying. Surely that is enough." Brother André looked up with pleading eyes. "Just five minutes more."

After fifteen minutes more the temporary porter was back in the chapel. "But, Brother, listen, I must go to my classes now," he urged. And then, with profuse apologies, but with eyes shining and happy, Brother André went back to his post.

Brother Ozée was always being asked to mind the door. "I'm just going to the village for a few minutes. I'll be back quickly," Brother André would promise. But often he was gone more than an hour. It was only later that Brother Ozée learned his sudden trip was made because he had just heard of some person who was very sick in the village and he wished to see him. Brother Ozée learned to be patient and say nothing, for Brother André had a way of making him feel he was helping, even if indirectly, with some important work.

Sometimes, when very tired and afraid he would fall asleep,

Brother André asked one of the Brothers who happened to be in the chapel at the time to wait until he was through and see he stayed awake. After a while the Brothers grew wary of these requests too, for Brother André never fell asleep, though his watchers often came close to it, so long did his prayer continue. After a while when someone in the chapel saw Brother André looking too intently at him, he immediately became very busy with his own prayers so that the porter's eyes and his would not meet.

Harassed with fatigue, especially on Wednesday and Saturday evenings, when after a day's work he imposed on himself the task of brushing the floor of the chapel, the porter accomplished his exercises of piety when the others were already in bed. In the darkness of the nave, his prayers rolled out—he knew them all by heart. If he fell asleep, he began them all over again when he woke up, and sometimes this heroic struggle lasted until next morning.

That their porter spent much of his night in the chapel the Community did not know for some time. But one night he gave himself away. He fell asleep there and when he started up he saw through the small round window communicating with the room above the apse a ray of light. He imagined he heard a noise and was so alarmed that he woke one of the Brothers by whispering at his bedside, "Come with me, Brother, there are thieves in the Chapel."

They hurried there together and Brother André was abashed to discover that the light was only the moon looking in at the window at the indefatigable Brother who had stayed too long and fallen asleep. He was very careful after that, for he did not want to risk having his visits curtailed. For the same reason he said nothing about his continual stomach trouble. Now and then the doctor insisted on a short rest, but the rest was always as brief as Brother André could make it.

Once a Brother took it upon himself to lock the door of the chapel to keep Brother André from going there at night. He concealed himself back of a door so he might see what the porter would do. To his amazement Brother André opened the door as if it were unlocked. When other members of the Community had heard of the incident they only laughed at the Brother for his naiveté and told him he must have forgotten to lock the door.

When Brother André was asked just how he managed to pray for such long hours of every day and night, he said there was nothing surprising about it. "When I am tired of being on my knees I stand up, and when I am tired of standing, I go back on my knees." But as a rule the Brothers, busy men that they were, paid little attention to Brother Porter. They knew he fulfilled his duties well, that he was a very pious soul, and that was enough for them.

The boys came often to the little man who was so kindly and pleasant, always willing to listen to their troubles, and ready to help them when he could. At first only a few took to the fact that he did actually seem able to help them. With the natural thoughtlessness of the young, there could be little to interest the boys in the quiet diminutive man who opened and closed doors and brought messages to them. But the small home-sick boys whom he helped over their nostalgia kept drifting into his office and talking to him, even after they felt better. When he noticed the sad eyes and lips of some newcomer that could not help trembling, he would ask gently, "You are not happy?"

The lad would nod or perhaps shake his head. The porter would go on with his gentle talk and after a few moments the kind face and the sympathetic manner made the boy forget his longing for home and he would join his mates in a better mood.

One day a discussion arose in front of his office regarding a new football. The old one was worn beyond hope but the

Brothers had said thriftily it would have to do until next season. The boys passed it from hand to hand, gloomily shaking their heads. Brother André came out of his office to ask what was wrong.

"Look, Brother, at this old football! We must have a new one and Brother Bursar says we can't. We may lose the game on account of it."

Brother André handled the worn brown oval. "It is pretty shabby," he agreed. "Perhaps Brother Bursar will change his mind. Go ask him again."

The boys looked at each other and shook their heads. But the boy who had been holding the ball went up the hall with it to the bursar's office. A few minutes later he came back and looked at Brother André, who had been standing silently as if he had forgotten that the second request had been his suggestion.

"He says we can have it," he said in awe. "It must have been you, Brother André—how did you do it?"

The little porter only ruffled the lad's hair. "You'll need a haircut soon, my boy," he said, and sent them all on their way. But as they were leaving triumphantly he called to them: "You might thank Saint Joseph for it. He is a very powerful patron, you know.

A few weeks later the matter of a picnic came up. The Brothers were insistent that every day was needed for attending classes during the rest of the term and there was not time to waste on an extra picnic. "Brother André got us the football," said one student. "Maybe he can get us the picnic." And, though a considerable number scoffed and laughed aloud at such an absurd idea, a small group went to the porter about the matter.

He listened gravely. "A picnic? But are you all so good in your studies as to deserve a picnic?"

They assured him they were. No boy could go on a picnic if he was back in his work. It was not that; it was the Brothers felt there was no spare time for picnics. "Well, we'll see," Brother André said and sent them away.

They went back to the others and were laughed at for their plans. Then at noon in the dining room there was an announcement. There would be a picnic after all. The matter of the work had been arranged. The boys looked at each other with shining faces. "He did it again," their eyes said to each other. But when they went to thank him, he waved them away with a smile. "Are you so sure I did it? Or was it Saint Joseph?" he asked with twinkling eyes.

After that the boys went to him with many requests. By no means all of their pleas were answered as they wished, but enough were to set Brother André in a very special place in their lives. Whenever they came to thank him, and to tell him how much they appreciated his power to accomplish the impossible for them, he always shook his head.

"What you might do is slip into the chapel and say a little prayer of thanks to Saint Joseph," he advised.

Sometimes he told them a story Father Provençal had told him long ago—the tale of the death of Saint Joseph, as related in an ancient Arab legend. As the Patriarch lay ill, his end near, Our Lord made him the promise that whoever told the history of His life and His trials and His separation from the world and put it in the words which Our Lord then spoke to His foster father, that person He would confide to Saint Joseph's care for all his life. And, added Our Lord, in the words of the legend: "When his soul deserts his body and he must needs quit the world I will burn the book of his sins and inflict no punishment on him in the day of judgment, but he will traverse the sea of fire without pain and without obstacle."

"And there," Brother André would say, his eyes shining,

"you can see how highly Our Lord esteemed Saint Joseph and how powerful he is."

Gradually the cult of Saint Joseph spread through the school. He began to be considered the patron saint of the student body—a thing which brought joy to the heart of his faithful client. For Brother André, of course, knew what the rest as yet only suspected. He knew that by himself nothing would be provided, but that it was his and the boy's whispered pleas to Saint Joseph that brought results.

When Brother André had been porter for some years and many boys had come and gone, each with his hair cut every month by the faithful religious while listening to murmured talk about the great saint of their land, one lad came whose face was pale, whose eyes were sunken.

"Are you sick, Jean?" asked Brother André.

"My head is splitting," Jean said weakly. "And worse luck, I have to study for an examination."

Brother André worked busily at the mop of hair for a while. He said nothing more until he had finished his job. Then, as the lad sat up straight in the chair, he asked him, "Is your head still so bad?"

Jean looked at him as if surprised at the question. "My head? Why it feels fine. The pain is all gone. What luck!" Then, as he started for the door, he came back again. "I forgot to pay you," and he handed the porter a nickel. He stared at Brother André for a moment with wondering eyes, then grinned. "You haven't asked me to do it yet, but to please you I'll say a prayer to Saint Joseph about my headache—but thank you just the same."

In his office Brother André put the coin with the others which he was hoarding so carefully. No one knew what he was planning to do with the money. In his own mind a plan was forming. Day after day as he sat in his office looking out across the street at the wild mountain opposite, he worked on his plan. It would have to be a very humble one, he knew, for after all nickels do not come to a great sum over the years. And a rough mountain does not offer much hope to make a dream come true. But he knew he had a powerful helper for his dream.

What he planned, as he sat in his tiny cubicle, or when he counted over the slowly growing pile of coins, was a place on that mountain where Saint Joseph would have a sanctuary of his own, a small chapel perhaps where the authorities would give permission for the Blessed Sacrament to be reserved some day, so that the saint could there watch over his foster Child again in his own house, as he had done years and years ago. For Brother André knew that that was what Saint Joseph wanted most of all.

He stood looking out of the door at the tangle of bush and outcropping stone. With his mind's eye he saw a small building and a road leading up to it. He was not at all sure how he was to get there. But obviously a saint who will aid a client in healing a boy's headache will aid him to secure a house for his Son.

CHAPTER THREE

THE LITTLE SHRINE ON MOUNT ROYAL

ON a pleasant spring day in 1890 ten-year-old Henri, a day pupil at the school, a lad who sometimes acted as aid to Brother André by posting the school letters for him in the village, came up to him with curious eyes.

"Brother André," he asked, "where were you going yesterday when it was getting dark? I saw you going right up the mountain."

Brother André nodded. "Yes, I went up there to pray to Saint Joseph. It is so quiet on the mountain. Prayers can be said there more easily, I think.

"Do you always go up there alone, Brother?"

"Yes, would you like to come up with me today?"

"Oh, I should love to, Brother. I'll ask my mother."

"Of course you must do that first. Then if she permits it, meet me right after supper."

There was a little footpath up the lower part of the mountain and they climbed it together until they came to a small clearing, a flat space, from which point the mountain began to climb more steeply. Together they knelt beside a great oak.

"Henri, pray with me for something I want very much," Brother André said. "At the foot of this tree I have buried a medal of Saint Joseph. Now pray with me that some day we shall be able to buy this land for him."

They came down the path together and, as they separated at the street, Brother André said confidently to the little boy, "We will get it—this piece of land, my child. Saint Joseph needs it."

Henri's mother and father and the other fathers and mothers of many of the pupils knew a great deal about Brother André by this time; more perhaps than the Brothers with whom he lived. He had whimsical qualities which they liked, but sometimes were impatient about. The bursar, for instance, found that every time Brother André put in order the articles on his desk a little statue of Saint Joseph was placed in a prominent place and always facing one way.

"Why do you always move this statue and put it facing that way, Brother?" he asked at last.

"You see Saint Joseph wants to be honoured on the mountain up there, Brother Bursar, and so I place him where he may look at it all day."

By this time everyone knew something of Brother André's hope, and most of them smiled indulgently when it was mentioned. But smiles or frowns, the hope remained in Brother André's mind always and on his tongue often.

One day a visitor came to the village and told of her sister's child who had been ill and who was well again right after Brother André had come in to see her and talk with her. "He is a saint," she told the Brother to whom she related her story. "He is truly a saint for he can heal the sick." A little while later something happened that several in the college saw with their own eyes. Brother André was busily mopping up the floor of the parlour when a woman, being helped along by two men, almost knocked his pail over.

"I'm so sorry, Brother. It's this lameness of mine," she apologized. "I have come to speak to Brother André about it."

The porter straightened up. "I'm Brother André." The cloth dripped on the floor unheeded as he looked closely at her. "Are you really lame? I think you can walk alone if you try. At least go as far as the chapel and see."

Her eyes still on his face, she stood up more erect, then

turned and walked haltingly, her attendants on each side ready to catch her. She went into the chapel with them and Brother André went back to his floor mopping. When she came out a little while later her face was tear stained but there was no halt in her step as she came to Brother André, who was wringing out the mop in one corner of the parlour.

"Brother, I heard you could heal—but now I know you can. I thank you from the bottom of my heart for your help. One of the boys told me you help people to walk, and so I came. And now I know you do heal."

He shook his head almost sternly. "No, madame, I can't heal. But Saint Joseph can—and evidently has."

"But I am so grateful. Can't I do something to help?"

At that he smiled. "Oh, yes, you can pray that some day Saint Joseph may have a good home for his Son up on the mountain there." And he pointed to the wild scene across the road. She looked at it for a while and then back at the little porter. "If he has you to help him, there is no doubt but he will have it."

Now the Community learned that on his trips to the village Brother André often stopped at the house of someone he had heard was ill, to talk a short while about Saint Joseph, and perhaps to bring the sufferer some of the oil from the lamp which burned in the little college chapel in front of Saint Joseph's statue.

Occasionally he was even called for while he was on duty as porter. One day he asked a young Brother to take charge for him so that he might see someone. He was gone longer than he had expected to be, with the result that Father Louage, the Superior, found no one in the house to answer when he rang the bell. When Brother André came back, he found the house in an uproar, and on Brother André fell the full displeasure of the Superior, who was known to have a quick temper. It fell on him so often in fact, that during those days religious in the house used to call Brother André the "lightning rod of the college" because the thunderbolts usually fell on him and so spared them. Brother André was very humble about it, for he knew it had been wrong to leave his post, and the young man left in charge had to go to other duties. He was not able to explain to the Superior's satisfaction just why he had done it, since he was certainly no doctor, and there was a good physician in the village to visit the sick.

Gradually the story of the little porter who could heal spread beyond the townspeople, as boarders took stories home with them. When parents came to visit, it was Brother André they asked for, to talk to and often to beg him to keep a watch over their sons. Sometimes, too, one of them came with a trouble of his or her own to the kindly little man whose eyes could narrow with mirth or grow wide with sympathy.

It was not so much that he accomplished any physical thing for them, but he made them feel that now all would be well. And always, of course, somewhere in every conversation, the talk would turn to Saint Joseph and his power and his love, and the house that might some day be built for him on the mountain.

There were other things that happened to Brother André during those years, and of these he said little. But one evening after he had returned from the village where he had prepared a body for burial (another request that came to him often) he went first to the chapel to say his prayers; then to his own room. Suddenly in the refectory he heard a crash of glasses and plates. He and a Brother who heard the clatter ran into the dining room, only to find everything intact and in its proper place. Brother André shook his head and tried to explain to the amazed and annoyed Brother: "Every time I lay out a corpse this happens afterwards. Always such a terrible noise!"

He grew confidential. "Sometimes I have seen what causes it too. A great big animal like a black cat. Do you think it is the devil who doesn't want me to run on errands of mercy?"

The Brother patted his worried confrère on the back soothingly. "No doubt," he said, "no doubt. Now go back to bed." But Brother André was on his way to the chapel again.

It was his custom to suggest to those who came to him in trouble that they start a novena to Saint Joseph, and he promised his own aid in prayer. As the years passed, more and more novenas were being said to Saint Joseph, and that the Brother hailed with joy. With equal joy he realised that these people who came to ask his prayers were a great and growing means of spreading devotion to his patron. He himself might offer to pray, offer to help—but the suppliants' prayers were the really important thing. He was merely the suggester, the adviser : that he never failed to insist on.

For some years these visitors who came to see Brother André had been merely superstitious people to many who had heard tales about remarkable favours granted through the little porter. The Brothers and the authorities, however, had not paid much attention to the talk, for Brother André was so good with the boys that his devotion made up for the inconvenience of having their doorkeeper occasionally away from his post. Besides, many of the parents approved of him highly. And he was such a good man, so full of pious zeal, so anxious to serve and to help, that there was really nothing to find fault with had they wanted to do so.

Suddenly they realised that the whole situation was changing rapidly. They saw the single visitors had become a group, and the group was becoming a crowd, as sick and lame from various parts of Montreal began coming to the college for help from the man who tended the door. Sometimes he took parties of them into the chapel with him. "Does he think he is leading

a pilgrimage?" asked one of the religious who did not approve
of all this.

The dusty roads of summer, the snowy roads of winter that
led to Côte-des-Neiges became sometimes crowded with those
who came for the advice and the prayers of the Holy Cross
porter. He had not changed his method of receiving them just
because they were more numerous. He still listened very quietly
and then he told them the one message he had to give them
all. He urged that the power of the mighty Saint Joseph be
invoked through prayer, and he always promised to add his
own to their prayers. Not only Catholics came to the door.
Protestants began to come, and to them too he gave the same
message. He sent them all away, better in heart and mind even
though a bodily cure might not have been brought about. But
accounts of actual bodily cures persisted, and increasingly more
of them as the years passed. By this time the groups had grown
large enough to come to the troubled attention of the authorities,
who after all were mainly interested in making the college a
place where boys were educated. The press became aware that
the college was a real news centre. Feature stories were printed ;
and this did not serve to lessen the number of those who came
to Côte-des-Neiges, some now out of mere curiosity, many to
get help for infirmities physical or spiritual.

Then, too, the college authorities could not close their eyes
any more to what was going on in the college itself. Not picnics
or new footballs now; nor an aching tooth relieved, but greater
things. There was the bursar, in bed with a broken leg and
with every prospect of still being there on Saint Joseph's feast
day, a day he longed so much to commemorate. He said so
sorrowfully to Brother André, busy in the infirmary. The latter
told him encouragingly, "Have faith and make the novena and
go down without fear on that day." And on the feast day there
was Brother Bursar in the chapel with the rest.

There was the boarder ill with a malignant fever to whom the infirmarian, going his rounds, said, "What are you doing here, you lazy boy?"

"I'm sick, Brother."

"Get up, get up."

"The doctor says I must stay here until the fever is gone."

"Never mind that. You are not sick any more. Go out for recreation."

The doctor objected to this counter order. "But the boy isn't sick," said Brother André. "Examine him—you will see he is well." The irritated doctor could find no trace of fever or any other sign of illness, though he came to look at the boy several times during the day.

Once there was a terrible outbreak of smallpox at Saint Laurent of which some died. When Brother André came to take his turn at nursing, he began by falling on his knees and praying Saint Joseph to remove the scourge. No further cases broke out, and there were no added deaths.

There is the incident of the surly man to whom the porter, back at the college on Mount Royal, said, "And how are things going at home?" The visitor stared at the smiling little porter. "What is that any business of yours?" he demanded. But after he had spent some time with the sons he had come to visit, he said apologetically to Brother André when he was leaving, "You see my wife has been ill in bed for a long time and she is worse now. That is why I am in such bad humour."

"Oh, she isn't as sick as you think," said Brother André reassuringly. "And she is very anxious to have you come home and tell her all about the boys. In fact, she is better at this very moment."

The man went away shaking his head. "Of all the odd prophets!" He meant to tell the story to amuse his wife when he got to her bedside. But when he reached home she herself met him at the door, still pale from illness, a worried nurse close behind her. "I'm well, I'm well," she called. And the days that followed proved she really was.

Of course, the stories of these cures were often much enlarged when they were told and retold. And the more they were repeated, the more numerous the sufferers that came crowding at the doors of Notre Dame College. And down in the village people were repeating even more than they used to, though still somewhat timidly, "You know, good Brother André at the college—he is a saint—he cures sick people."

The matter grew increasingly worrisome. For one thing, all the Brothers were needed for work, and the many visitors took Brother André away from his duties, and more and more often he had to have a substitute. And now some of the boys' parents began complaining about the old doorkeeper with his supernatural powers, and said it was not supernatural but superstitious. And all these sick people around their children—something must be done or they would take their boys elsewhere.

Friends of the Community began to receive protests and advice. If—so ran the gist of them—these ever increasing pilgrimages to Brother André were allowed to continue, then the Congregation of Holy Cross was soon going to be placed in a ridiculous position, one that would hurt religion as well as the Congregation itself.

In the Community there was divided opinion about these crowds of visitors for whom Brother André was the chief attraction. Complaints began to pile up on the Provincial, who was among those who had watched Brother André for some years and who considered him a very saintly religious. Some went to the archbishop with their fears for the future of the Faith if this lay Brother were not prevented from continuing his mischief. The archbishop listened carefully to both sides, those eager to stop Brother André's work and those eager to have his work receive episcopal recognition. For several years he said nothing officially about the matter at all, but watched developments at the college.

Many of those who felt that Brother André was honest and inspired were indignant when they learned what was being said about the little Brother. They knew of his work and the favours granted through him, and they were curious to know just what harm could come from the devotion of a simple religious to the saint who was the head of the Holy Family itself. When, ran the demand, did the Catholic Church ever forbid the faithful to honour and pray to Saint Joseph, and in any way they wished? They added that the enemies of so holy a man must be enemies of the Church too. Among his defenders were Protestants and Jews, who had seen him and talked with him and now offered any aid needed for his defence. When they came to tell him so, he said the same thing to all their offers. "But I have no enemies. How can I have? I am unimportant. And surely if my superiors feel the complaints are justified they will order me to stop receiving pilgrims."

He paid little attention to the controversy, probably hearing of it only when some indignant friends spoke of it. He went on quietly meeting his visitors, praying and looked longingly at the wooded slope where more than one medal now lay buried at the foot of the oak tree, in that flat space that would so nicely provide a small house for Saint Joseph and his Son.

He was too happy in his religious life to note outsiders' disputes. A few years before in a letter to the Nadeaus (his aunt's family) he had outlined the ideal of his life : "What greater good fortune and happiness could there be than the religious life? So laborious in appearance but so happy in reality! Now there is left me only to ask Providence to call others of the family to this happy lot."

The little Brother, often sick, but always smiling, full of

laughter and tears, held to this ideal as he held to his dream—
his dream of some work for Saint Joseph, to whom since baby-
hood he had prayed and who, he was positive, was responsible
for his journey that had ended at Mount Royal.

Each day he went over to the mountain now, if only for a
few moments. He loved mountains, far away from the world's
noise. Up there one was close to God. It was like a mighty
prie-dieu, he thought, a mountain.

His work as porter and the constantly growing crowds of
people come to see him made a long weary day for him. The
mountain now was an escape for him as well as a place of
prayer. In the little clearing he had fashioned a sort of shrine
to Saint Joseph, purchased with some of his hoarded nickels.
In order that it should not be too exposed to the elements,
he had managed to arrange the stones so that a flat one was
over the saint's head.

The little twisting path that led to it was known to only a
few people, so no pilgrims followed him there. He could be
alone for a few stolen moments sometimes in the afternoon.
These he spent in prayer, with the late sunlight on his small,
black-clad figure. Every day there were more and more people
to pray for—people who at the foot of the mountain had
brought him their burden of pain of body and soul.

Sometimes when he was ready to go down the path again
he would stand for a little while and look about him : at the
soft green of oaks and birches and maples, at the darker pines
and firs, and past them to the plain where far off the Laurentians
were blue in the distance. He would dream of a day when Saint
Joseph in a real house would watch over the college from this
summit, and over the little villages that dotted the flat land
between this mountain and the distant ranges. Brother André
had hope and he had faith, and he could pray very long and
very hard. He knew he could afford to wait. He still talked

about it to all the boys when he cut their hair, and he prayed
continually in the chapel for the fulfilment of his dream.

* * *

There was a *Sacré Coeur* on the Mount of Martyrs in Paris,
and high in the Pyrenees was a shrine to Our Lady, Brother
André used to say—"and why not a Mount Royal to Saint
Joseph?"

He had interested the novices in the little shrine, and often
on holidays they made for the mountains, sitting and talking
together in the space before the shrine, and reciting the Office
of the Blessed Virgin in front of it. And more than one had
buried a medal there.

The college was very anxious to own the property now, but
not, alas, for the reason for which Brother André wanted it.
The land had been originally owned by an ill-tempered man
who sometimes objected to anyone going up there and
threatened to set his dogs on visitors. He wanted to sell the
land, but his price was high; and there were no purchasers
since there was no real reason for buying. The religious heard
that a sort of road house would be built there if it were sold,
and they began to worry about the possibility of such a place
so close to their college. However, all negotiations failed. Then
suddenly it was sold and again put on the market, but again
the price was beyond the means of the Community.

One day Brother Alderic, the bursar whose broken leg had
healed so rapidly through Brother André's prayers, climbed the
path to add one more medal to the collection in the ground.
As if this last medal were the one necessary thing for success,
news came suddenly that the land about the mountain facing
the college had been bought by the religious of Holy Cross.
The owner had come down in his price, the religious had been

able to go somewhat higher than their original offer, and at last, in July of 1896, the property came into the hands of the Community.

When Brother André heard about Brother Alderic's medal, he smiled happily. "Such an act of faith in our Patron I consider an excellent means of evicting unruly proprietors."

The Community now owned eighteen acres, mostly covered with timber. It was a rectangular piece of ground extending from Queen Mary road to the top of the mountain. No one thought it would ever be of much use, but perhaps the lower part could be put in some sort of shape and used for cultivation. The rugged hillside could be left as it was ; the flat promontory halfway up might serve as a playground and recreational centre for students and faculty.

Brother André now looked out of his porter's cell with happy eyes at the big mountain which was coming into what he and Saint Joseph had planned for it. When a small kiosk was built there and a rustic path leading to it, with occasional steps to break the steep ascent, he looked even happier. And though some people laughed at the grandiose name "Saint Joseph's Boulevard" which the students had given to the path, Brother André saw in it a prophecy more than a name.

The Brother did not know much history, but there was one page of Canada's story he knew and cherished—the story of how, as far back as 1642, when danger from the rising St. Lawrence threatened, and "Villa Maria" inhabitants were in sore straits, Maisonneuve, governor of the fort, promised that if his people were spared, he would carry a cross and plant it on the crest of Mount Royal in thanksgiving. The waters fell and the governor fulfilled his promise. So, from the beginning Mount Royal had been a place of blessing and promise.

Brother André began in his spare moments to widen the little path up the hill ; at first by himself, later with helpers.

The small pavilion built of tough timbers was a pleasant place to sit on a sunny afternoon. The roof was so flat that by climbing a ladder placed against the wall, one could stand there and look over the shining landscape.

He himself kept careful eye on every little improvement, though, of course, improvements so far had been made entirely for the college. In a crevice of rock near the pavilion where he now set his statue of Saint Joseph, he placed also a little dish to receive the donations of any casual visitor who might climb there. Also when he himself had visitors now, he generally managed to bring the conversation round to the new pavilion on Mount Royal and the excellent view obtainable from there. And while they were sightseeing, he added, they might say a little prayer before the statue of Saint Joseph. He did not mention the dish waiting for contributions. In fact, he was not quite sure just yet what he meant to build or when, but he knew the little dish with its coins would swell the fund for the future work which the haircuts had begun.

He had what he considered the beginning of a building. He had been given a large statue of Saint Joseph which he put carefully away. After all, no foundation stone could be more necessary, no keystone more basically important to the building of his dream than a statue of Saint Joseph.

He spoke occasionally to the authorities about the great desirability of some sort of chapel on the hill, but the request was refused over and over because of the expense. There was an additional reason not mentioned to Brother André : if such a building were projected by the Congregation of Holy Cross, it might be interpreted as giving official recognition to something which had thus far been merely tolerated. For, as the cures effected through the prayers of Brother André became more frequent and more talked about, so also did objections to his apostolate wax louder. Authorities in the Community wished matters to remain quiet and as they were, and a chapel erected at Côte-des-Neiges might increase the volume of criticism.

Brother André at times grew heartsick with waiting. Here was this lovely land theirs at last, here was Saint Joseph needing a place where his pilgrims could come in his honour and for his help. And nothing was done. His small store of coins was growing ; but he knew he needed much more for such a project, although he had little idea just how much.

Suddenly Saint Joseph himself showed Brother André the way. The porter was quite ill and the doctor had ordered him to the infirmary for a few days' rest. Brother André had stayed there one day. The next morning the doctor found him in the parlour washing windows. "You'll be dead in two months if you don't get some rest," the physician warned him.

Brother André wrung out the cloth in the pail. "Oh, well," he said, his eyes twinkling, "if I die the Community will be well rid of me." But he went back docilely enough to the infirmary to rest some more.

Father Lecavalier, the Superior, was the only other patient there at the time. The two talked together a good deal, for neither was very ill, and naturally the favourite subject of Brother André's conversation was Saint Joseph, to whom the Superior also had a great devotion. The Brother saw his chance. Breathlessly he poured out his plans and hopes and begged the Superior to give him permission to build a little chapel on the mountain. "A very little one," he promised. "Not even windows would be necessary," he emphasized.

The Superior was intrigued. But there was always one unfailing objection to such work in a community that needed its money. "The cost, Brother André—I don't know."

"Oh, I have a little sum. And the carpenter here would help me to build it. With the two hundred I have saved—if you will authorize its use—I could build most of it with that.

And more will come." By the time the two patients left the infirmary, Brother André had permission both for spending his money and for the services of the community carpenter.

As soon as he spread the joyous news it became clear that he was by no means the only one who wanted a chapel built on the mountain. Many of the people who had come to him at the college and who had prayed with him in the college chapel, made themselves into a sort of unofficial committee to begin collecting contributions to swell the building fund.

All this seemed to come in the very nick of time. Hostile voices were growing louder; some of the parents were objecting very loudly to the sick and afflicted who were permitted to crowd the school corridors at all hours of the day; and those who came to visit their sons often had to mingle with the invalids come to see the porter. Finally the authorities ordered Brother André not to receive any pilgrims in future during parlour hours at the school.

The good works of Brother André had mounted to the dignity of a problem, even for those who thoroughly approved of his apostolate. The Community had to be very careful not to have discredit brought upon it through a religious known to be illiterate and eccentric, though he was also known to be very zealous. On the other hand, they knew that so much good had been accomplished by him, they did not wish in any way to seem guilty of thwarting the designs of Providence. The spirit of faith kept them from opposing his work directly, but they did consider the advisability of sending Brother André to another house—the University of St. Joseph in New Brunswick —only to discard that idea later on.

When his superior called on the Archbishop of Montreal, who had been told about the whole matter again and again by both sides, he asked, "Would Brother André stop receiving the sick if you told him to?"

"I am sure he would obey kindly," declared his Superior.

"Then let him alone. If his work is from God it will live; if not it will crumble away."

So, for the time being, those of his confrères, the village doctor and the other lay sceptics who openly opposed him were held in check. But it hurt his friends to the quick to hear him called "a fake healer and a quack doctor." Brother André was hurt by it too, but he never wasted much time coddling emotions. When the visiting hours at the school were closed to his pilgrims, and he was given the use of a store across the street to receive them, he spent no time in repining. He merely went across the street and arranged affairs in the cramped space put at his disposal.

The store was opposite the college, and in it M. Sauvage and his wife sold religious articles and ran a little restaurant. One corner of the store was given to Brother André for his office and another corner as a waiting room for his visitors. They overflowed into the street before long and the situation was not much remedied. What saddened Brother André was that now the infirm and crippled had to wait in the open tramway shed or even in the street until there was room for them inside.

One day there were so many he stood back of the Sauvage counter and asked each in turn what was wanted. To everyone he gave the same instructions : say the novena, apply the oil, and the medal. Suddenly he caught sight of one sick man, leaning on two crutches at the back of the room. "Give me your crutches," he demanded, leaning forward to get his direct attention. "You can walk. Do it!"

As the crowd turned from their own troubles to stare at his pointing finger, they heard the crutches drop to the floor, and saw the man step forward haltingly, his eyes fixed unwaveringly on Brother André. He was so moved he could only stare at the lay Brother, tears pouring down his cheeks. Then, as if mad with joy, he ran for the door and jumped into a passing tram.

Brother André smiled and stopped the murmur rising about him. "It is not that he is ungrateful. He has good news to take home." And he went back to his work. That night some of his confrères found him sitting silently in his office. "What is troubling you, Brother?" one of them asked.

He looked at them with clouded eyes. "It is only that—you see I am so vile an instrument—to touch them and know they will be well—that God does it through me—that Saint Joseph wants me—it frightens me sometimes."

For besides the man with the crutches there had been another remarkable happening that day. Polydor Beaulne, a young workman, limping badly, had come to the college and said hesitatingly to Brother Bursar as he stood at the office door, "I've come from the village to see if Brother André will help me. But the store is already so crowded! Do you think there will be any way of my seeing him? I can't stand and wait, you see."

"Wait over there in the little parlour. He is almost due to come back and then you can stop him on his way to the chapel." The man waited.

Brother André came hurrying so fast, he had gone by before the sick man could stop him. He limped after him and put a hand on his shoulder. "Brother André, you are my prisoner."

The little Brother stopped, smiled and pretended to spar with him. "And what do you want over here?"

"Brother, I've hurt my leg and I cannot work. And I've got a big family to take care of."

Brother André looked at him in pretended astonishment. "Hurt? You? Nonsense! You're nothing but a lazy fellow. Walk—go ahead! You can do it easily."

Beaulne took a few steps and found he did not need his stick
any more. His leg felt as strong as ever. He was so bewildered
he could only stare and murmur, "You are right, Brother
André. I can walk."

"Of course you can," came the businesslike voice. "And now
let's go into the chapel together and pray a little to Saint
Joseph."

Some, however, continued to call him an old meddler and
charlatan, even though there was no open objection at all to
his work. Brother André, of course, gave of his help freely to
anyone who asked for it, rich or poor, friend or enemy. One
doctor had been for some years bitterly engaged in fighting
him with a zeal worthy of a better cause and had done all he
could to stand in the way of his work and reputation. Then
his wife became the victim of uncontrollable haemorrhages.
Her husband called in his wisest confrères but they could do
nothing. His wife said to him feebly, "I've a great favour to
ask. I didn't do it before, but now you see your science is
powerless to help me. Please go to Brother André because I
feel certain he can help me."

The doctor hesitated between pride and love, but the latter
finally won and Brother André was sent for. Hardly had the
Brother crossed the room, hardly had the woman given him a
look of trust and faith, than she was definitely cured.

This was only one case of an enemy seeing the light. Others
kept on. Since they were not able to bring the archbishop to
take any action against the porter, they turned to the civil
authorities. "The public health is at stake," was the burden of
their complaints. Hundreds of little boys were in danger and
their parents too ; for even though the sick had been forbidden
to come to the college at certain hours, there were still hours
left for them to come.

So a delegate from the Board of Health came to see Brother

André, who received him courteously and listened to his reasons for the official call. The Brother carefully explained to the man exactly what he was doing, showed him the medals and the oil which his clients made use of. The official was able to assure himself there was nothing in all this against health regulations. He went back with a report that there was absolutely no need of an investigation, and stated that the one most noticeable thing in the interview and examination was Brother André's great fund of common sense.

His enemies tried another approach. This time they struck at his reputation. They said he was guilty of immodesty because of the way he touched the sick. Some, in fact, sent persons to see him who were urged to ask him to touch them, evidently with the idea of bringing charges against him. When this last report came to his ears, and he realized that even his own Community was beginning to worry, Brother André went to a layman who had appeared to be sympathetic with his work. To this layman he opened his heart, telling him various signal proofs he had received of Saint Joseph's aid—facts he had never before shared with anyone.

This layman, instead of feeling honoured at these confidences and keeping them secret, spread abroad the report that the porter was a poor fool. This was something that had never happened to Brother André before. He knew he had enemies and critics as he knew he had friends. But he had never before been betrayed by one he had thought his friend. With the surprise of a hurt child, he said in utter bewilderment, when he heard of the betrayal, "Why he has repeated everything that I told him!"

On the evening he had learned of this, he came sadly into his little office at the college and found he had a visitor. "You must go across the street," the Brother began mechanically ; then he looked more closely. "But this is little Henri—and grown big!" he exclaimed.

The young man was leaning on the arm of a comrade. He turned to his companion. "I told you he would remember me," he said triumphantly.

"Of course I do," said Brother André. "You are the lad who was the very first to go up to the mountain with me years ago. But you are ill. You look so very pale."

"Oh, it was an accident. I came to you because my left leg is gangrenous and the doctor says I must go to the hospital ; and probably have it amputated. So I came to you. You can cure me, can't you, Brother ?"

Brother André shook his head. "Oh, no, I can't. But no doubt Saint Joseph can if you have faith. Now let your friend take the carriage you came in and go home. You stay here. There is a little room next to my office, which you shall have for a while."

Later he went to see the young man, after his porter duties were finished, and found him in bed looking paler and sicker than ever. Brother André took the cover from the bed, looked long and earnestly at the swollen leg, black with disease. He rubbed it gently, silently, smiling encouragement at the young man. For a long time the Brother sat thus, still and recollected, and always rubbing the injured leg.

By late evening the limb was so sound and whole that the young man walked home to the village, unaided over slippery snow. He was shaking with excitement, but his leg was as well as it had been when as little Henri he trudged up the hill with the same Brother André beside him to put a medal under the oak tree.

Brother André watched him until he had disappeared from sight down the road, then went into the chapel to give thanks. He felt happy again. What did calumniating tongues matter when Saint Joseph was healing through his client's humble prayers ?

Chapter Four

THE FIRST MIRACLES

It was near the end of the summer of 1904 that Father Superior had given permission to Brother André to use the services of Brother Abondius, the carpenter, and authorized his spending the two hundred dollars he had saved. Brother Abondius' labours were to be entirely free. The money was to be used to build a small chapel, eighteen by fifteen feet and to pay for the timber and the services of additional workmen who might be needed.

Of course a foundation had to be dug first of all. While several workmen were digging a space for the building, and as Brother André was watching them during the days when the work was begun, a young man came up the walk and greeted him. "Remember me, Brother?"

Brother André smiled. "Of course I do. You are Polydor Beaulne. Are you quite well now? Is the leg all right?"

Beaulne assured him it was. "I've come to ask you if you need a mason to help build your foundation here."

"Indeed I do. But the money—there is so little and it may not come in every week."

"I'll take a chance on that, Brother. You helped me. It's my turn now. Shall I start right in?"

Brother André liked Beaulne and often came to talk to him. One day the Brother appeared holding a book in his hand which he showed proudly—a copy of *The Following of Christ.* "You know I am not educated at all. When I came here I could scarcely read or write. What I know the Fathers have taught me. I can read quite easily now."

The building grew under Brother André's watchful eyes. It had no windows at all, and the only light came from a double pane of glass on the roof. At the back, double folding doors exposed the whole inside to view, as would the doors of a barn. The opened doors served the purpose of admission to those of the pilgrims who could not get inside, and several rows of benches were placed for their convenience. It might be classified as the nave with only the sky for a vault.

It was late in the July of 1904 when Brother André and his small group of workmen had climbed the slope to begin their work. Before two months were over the two hundred dollars allowed to carry out the project were spent for wood and work-men's wages. However, the supply of money was replenished in due time and the work went on without interruption.

"Shall we come back on Monday?" the workmen would ask at the week's end.

"Well, I'm out of money," Brother André would usually say. "I haven't any more."

"We'll come anyway. If you haven't it by the end of the week we can wait."

Then during the month the money always came in. The little mite box beside what would one day be the chapel entrance was always found to contain enough to pay the workmen. The money came mainly from those persons who, some among them recipients of cures, had banded together informally to visit Brother André and pray with him on certain evenings in the college chapel. In a sense they made themselves promoters of the work, giving and collecting the funds. The rest came from small coins placed there by pilgrims who climbed the mountain to watch the work progress. So the original two hundred dollars had frequent and much needed additions. Not once were the workmen asked to wait for their wages at the end of the week.

For when the time came the mite box anyhow held enough for them, though often hardly a cent over.

* * *

While Brother Abondius and his men were working on the building, Brother André pondered how to build a wagon road to it. He knew the little trail, broadened already by the crowds, was much too narrow. He knew too, that such a project was beyond his own strength or his ability, and that any money that came in would have to be devoted to the chapel for some time to come.

One day as he was brooding over this new problem, seeing a young man climbing with some difficulty up the path to the spot where he was standing, he recognized Calixte Richard, elder brother of one of the students, come to visit his relatives.

"Can I do anything for you, Brother?" he asked, breathless from the climb. "You look worried."

"Yes, you could tell me how I can get a road built up here. The path is much too narrow, but I haven't the money or men to build it."

Calixte laughed. "Well, it happens that I am a quarry hand and could very well help you, but you see I am too sick to work. I have a bad dyspeptic condition and I've laid off from work till I get better."

Brother André looked at him closely. "You are thin; I can almost see through you. But come along and look over the job and perhaps you can give me some suggestions."

They walked together along the site of the proposed road. Suddenly Brother André stopped. "If Saint Joseph cures you, would you come and work for me?" he asked.

Calixte had not quite followed this sudden flight of the Brother. "I am really not able, Brother. I haven't the strength.

I would have to be able to eat good, big meals to do that."

Brother André repeated his question. "But if you were cured, would you help me?"

"Oh, of course in that case. But you see how impossible it is."

"I'll give you a good meal right now. Come along with me." He took the alarmed Calixte to the college and asked the cook to give food to the visitor. Then he stood over the young man and saw he ate it all. "How do you feel?" he asked.

"Fine now," was the answer; "but I'm afraid of how I'll feel later."

Hours later Calixte still felt all right, and Brother André took him up the mountain again. "Now come along and get to work."

Calixte began to work, feeling in fact as well as he had ever been; and the man who had not worked for three years, because of illness, took up the difficult task of quarrying a road in the mountain. Not until the day the road was finished did Calixte miss a day's work.

One day a carter delivering a load of lumber came up to Brother André, puffing from his climb. "My horse won't come up your steep incline, Brother. I have tried kindness and I've tried beating. He won't move."

Brother André looked at him, then beyond him. "But isn't that your horse right behind you?"

The carter turned; there was the stubborn animal at the chapel. He looked back to the street dazed, not quite sure if it were really his horse. He shook his head and stared at the little Brother; then smiled mischievously. "I guess this is one of those miracles they tell of"; and still shaking his head, he began unloading the lumber.

The dedication of the chapel took place in mid-November of 1904. In honour of the formal opening, Brother André donned his new habit, a concession usually reserved for Christmas.

The statue of Saint Joseph, which had been an early gift, was blessed in the college chapel and then carried in procession up Calixte's fine new road to the little sanctuary. Holy Mass was celebrated; and later the Stations of the Cross were erected. Brother Abondius had built the little white altar that looked very festive with candles and bright flowers. Saint Joseph must have felt very much at home, for surely the little house at Nazareth was never more simply furnished than this small new home which bore his name.

Up the road with the others came the porter who had planned it all, the joy of accomplishment anchored in his heart. He was almost sixty years old now, a thin little man whose hair was getting grey, but who had in his erect carriage, in his smile, and in his twinkling eyes an air of youth. He had been troubled and saddened by the attitude of many, some even in his own Community, toward his work, but today that did not matter. Today he could turn his whole mind to the accomplished fact that stood before him as he marched—a little house of God with no windows, not much over fifteen feet square in size, with no regular doors at all. But it was a good thing the carpenters had so arranged it, since the side which faced the mountain could be thrown open; for the crowd which came for the ceremony needed all the extra space, and many stood in the open to hear Mass.

On that first day the congregation was made up of some of the priests and Brothers of the Congregation of Holy Cross, students and the men and women who had been interested in the project and had helped with it. Monsignor Racicot, vicar general of Montreal, blessed the chapel. Father Geoffrion offered Mass after the statue had been placed on the altar; a plain wooden affair, made by the loving hands of Brother Abondius, who certainly had skill beyond that of the ordinary carpenter. Flowers had been placed there by the devoted hands of Brother André himself.

The joy of seeing his chapel finished was short-lived. For hardly was it opened when it had to be closed again. There was not enough money to install any sort of heating facilities, so he would have to wait until spring to see another service there.

From his porter's cell he often looked longingly up at the mountain where Richard's road was plainly visible and the little house at the top where Saint Joseph waited alone. And sometimes when he went over to the room in M. Sauvage's store where the sick waited for him—for even in the cold Canadian winters there were always some who came—he took time to go up the mountain to see that all was well with the oratory, as he liked to call the chapel.

One evening some of the pilgrims lingered in the store. It was late when Brother André came out to them from the corner that was his office. Instead of turning to the college, he hesitated a moment, then looked toward the mountain and began to take the road up there instead.

"May we come too?" called one of the visitors.

He looked back. "If you like. I have some candles up there."

They climbed silently through the cool spring evening. When they stopped for a brief rest they saw behind them the lights of distant little towns that formed clusters of brightness in the dark. As they went on they had almost to feel their way, although Brother André was going sure-footedly ahead of them. They could hear, even though they could scarcely see him.

By the time they reached the chapel they saw inside the flicker of a candle. He came to the entrance shielding it with his hand. Then he put it on his prie-dieu and knelt there. They grouped themselves about him and all prayed together. Brother Abondius' altar shone white and Saint Joseph was faintly visible looking down at them.

"We will come with you again," several who lived in the

town told him when they had returned to the street. "Perhaps we can have a regular hour once a week up here instead of in the college chapel."

Brother André was pleased. "I know that a candle of this size lasts just about an hour. So we will light it and we can make the time a Holy Hour."

The group sometimes also joined him in the Stations of the Cross in the college chapel to his deep joy. For this devotion to the Passion was most deep-seated of all; Saint Joseph was for Brother André only the way to God. The Passion was the secret of his work.

He would lead the group from one station to the other, crucifix in hand, and in detail speak of Our Lord's sufferings—the beating, the cords, the crown of thorns pressed down on his head, the nails. Tears were often in his eyes, often rolled down his cheeks, and his grief was so real that it showed he was suffering at first hand his Lord's sufferings. More than one repentance, more than one conversion were traceable to these stations.

Later he would sometimes discuss with his visitors some of the lovers of the Passion about whom he had read, especially Catherine Emmerich and Saint Gertrude. Although he read very slowly, perhaps as fast as a normal ten-year-old boy, he remembered well and frequently repeated phrases from their works.

When there were no pilgrims and no friends present, just the same every evening, no matter how worn with work, he made the stations alone. His programme was definite. First he knelt close to the altar for an hour, with no support, lost to all about him. Then he slowly made each station, and it took him nearly another hour to complete the full round. Often the people with him, twice as strong as he, could not go through the devotion without sitting on a bench at intervals.

One who often came with him said of these stations : "Every time I make the Way of the Cross in his company I say to myself after hearing him improvise his long and moving prayers, he is like the Apostles who were ignorant fishermen, but who became inexhaustible preachers on the subject of Christ." It seemed to an observer that he never wanted to stop because he was so interested. And usually his prayers were like a conversation with one invisible. He listened to the answer and replied in another tone.

With the spring bringing warmer weather it also brought the pilgrims in increasing crowds. The name and fame of the little shrine were more and more widely known. Nearly every day there was a trickle of people climbing to the little chapel to pray, and on some days the trickle grew to a stream. Even in chilly weather they kept coming in rain, wind, snow flurries, to the little place of prayer. Brother André still kept up with his porter's work, but it was very light during the summer vacations and so he could sometimes devote almost his whole day to the sick, going straight from the chapel to the store and back again. But the duties which remained, he fulfilled faithfully.

Sometimes in the afternoon when he was busily raking the college lawn, he would not seem to see the pilgrims jostling him. Becoming aware that one of them was trying to talk to him, he would shake his head and say, "Go wait for me in the store or at the oratory. I will join you when I am free."

As summer came it was to the oratory that they usually went. And before long they had to wait until there was room to enter the little shrine, lighted only with the opening in the roof and the candles burning before Saint Joseph's statue. Some of them strolled through the woods—itself a quiet place for prayer and meditation. Some, the really well ones, climbed higher and showed each other the far-off Laurentians, the vast Montreal cemetery with its wide terraces, the Lake of Two Mountains, the Cistercian monastery with its great stone Calvary.

More and more often in the evenings he took a group to the chapel, with a lantern guiding their steps as they came down the road afterwards. The chapel had decorations now; grateful pilgrims who came back after a cure brought with them ex-voto offerings, little plaques; most of these were commonplace enough; but some of the little square offerings were beautifully lettered. And their messages had only one burden: "Here —— was cured and offers thanks to Saint Joseph." And along the wall were hung an increasing number of crutches and other aids to the crippled and sick. All were silent witnesses of pain past and happiness won by a cure.

Even by 1900 Brother André's reputation had spread so far that many insisted he had unusual powers. But when they came to analyse his work and his methods all they could say was that he exhorted them to pray to Saint Joseph, from whom any favour was possible, to touch themselves with his medal, to apply the oil; and he himself promised to add his prayers to theirs. In his porter's office, in the Sauvage store, in the village, and now in the small chapel, he said always and only, "Pray to Saint Joseph and he will help you." To hear these simple orders and to see the little humble lay Brother, brought more and more people to Mount Royal until it became evident some sort of organization was needed to care for them.

In 1905 the first organized pilgrimage to the Oratory was made. It was composed of a group of Montreal men and women who knew of Brother André's work at first hand. A second pilgrimage was led by Abbé Perault of the nearby Côte-des-Neiges parish. After that, pilgrimages occurred frequently. There was so little room for the pilgrims that one day when a bad storm came up, only a small part of the crowd could find shelter. It was clear that some sort of protection would have to be built. Not, however, until 1908 was one erected, and then it was merely a roof supported by posts which acted as an extension to the chapel itself. When a little later this was boarded up, it formed the nave of the church and the entire original chapel became the sanctuary. From then on, the Oratory was heated during the winter and pilgrims could come there all year round.

In 1906 Father George Dion, Provincial Superior of the Congregation, had moved his headquarters from Saint Laurent, where he had been pastor, to Notre Dame College. Here he could more carefully watch Brother André's work, in which he felt great interest and of which, to speak frankly, he had a certain amount of suspicion. He went there primarily to protect the Congregation from any possible over-zeal on the part of Brother André. But before he had been in residence long he became one of the porter's firmest supporters and was the man who was to prove the outstanding builder of the growing Oratory. Through the years he watched over Brother André and his work and the church that was growing on the mountain.

In the beginning there had been a certain amount of trouble. On Father Dion's first visit to the chapel he had looked with disfavour at the crutches that cluttered it, and ordered them removed. When Brother André heard about this he, for once, registered a strong protest. Fortunately Father Dion was a man of tact as well of authority. He listened carefully and patiently to Brother André's explanations ; then, deciding he had been wrong, ordered the crutches all set back again.

This was, of course, a small matter ; in a certain way it was important. It was much more of a victory than merely putting back the crutches. It was the first time an inquiry of any sort had been made by authority into Brother André's work, and the work had been sustained.

To many people Father Dion seemed cold ; and his dignified

bearing and his serious face overawed them. But Brother André was to find in him through the years a pillar of strength and a source of help that never failed. Father Dion had voluntarily approached a situation of great difficulty and one of which he himself at first doubted the necessity or final value. But assured of its merit and need, and that it was in entire conformity with the interests of religion, he remained steadfast through the years, proving to be the very man needed for this critical period. To Brother André money meant very little. He had thought two hundred dollars enough to build a church, and that outlook he carried along with him in every future development of the Oratory. Father Dion knew values and prices, and with him as administrator and builder, Brother André could stop worrying and serenely go on with his real work—the sick and the afflicted.

Occasionally this utter oblivion to the cost of things tried Father Dion's patience. Once, the Brother brought a cheque for five hundred dollars from a wealthy man in Montreal and presented it proudly to Father Dion with the remark, "Now we cna build a larger church." Father Dion, busy with many things, flashed back, "I suppose you will want a basilica next." There was a silence, and he looked up to see Brother André standing rapt and dreaming. Obviously Father Dion had unwittingly planted a new and wonderful thought in Brother André's head.

However, even though a basilica was no difficulty, Father Dion had to listen to frequent complaints from Brother André, usually relayed from the pilgrims, regarding the smallness of the Oratory and the need of further enlarging it. At last the Brother was given permission to make the chapel larger and better to increase his good work. However, Father Dion, though he had refused to be influenced by Brother André's detractors, felt that the time was not yet ripe for a definite decision and wanted to wait.

The following year a group of laymen went to Father Dion and urged him to see if he could get increased housing on the mountain. He promised he would take the matter up with the diocesan authorities. Later he and Brother André went to visit Monseigneur Bruchési, Archbishop of Montreal. Brother André waited quietly while Father Dion outlined the work which the friends of the lay Brother had put forward. When he had finished Monseigneur shook his head doubtfully. "It sounds like a very expensive enterprise." He turned to Brother André. "Don't you have any fears about undertaking it, Brother?"

Brother André answered respectfully but firmly, "No, your excellency—none at all."

The archbishop looked searchingly at the little man with the workworn hands, the shabby habit, the face of one born out of the working class. "Brother André, there is just one thing I want to ask you. Is there something of the supernatural in this which you are doing? Do you have visions of some sort? Is it Saint Joseph who told you he wanted a church on Mount Royal?"

"Oh, no, your excellency, no! It is nothing of that kind at all. It is only that I have a great devotion to Saint Joseph. That is what guides me and gives me confidence."

The archbishop promised to take the matter up with his diocesan council. Some weeks later Father Dion had their reply and his. Before permission for the erection of a public oratory such as was sought could be given, the archbishop must know the cost and must also insist that the sum be well guaranteed before the work was begun. Besides, there were so many diocesan works that the faithful had to support, he said he could allow no collections for the purpose. And such a building would belong to the College of Notre Dame when erected; and the Congregation of Holy Cross would have to be responsible for its maintenance. For a time matters remained at a standstill, since the laymen who were interested felt they must be very sure of funds before they began the work.

One summer day in 1908 a business man in Montreal decided, after being urged by his wife, to visit this little chapel on Mount Royal about which she had talked so much. And so many people had said to him, "Do you know Brother André? They say he works miracles," that he decided to go and see the place for himself.

His wife was delighted, for her husband had been very sceptical about the matter. They climbed the road bordered by trees, went into the little chapel and looked around. When they came out they saw Brother André himself coming toward them, stopping on his way to greet a few people who asked for his prayers. He approached the couple. "What can I do for you?"

"Brother André, my wife and I have come to recommend ourselves to your prayers."

"Is this the first time you have ever been here?"

"The first time for me, but my wife has been here often."

Brother André smiled at his visitors. "I am very glad you realise it is not necessary to be sick in order to come here and pray to Saint Joseph and place yourself under his protection. I hope you will come again."

That promise was made and kept through the years. "I have heard of Brother André for six or seven years from the people," he told his wife on their way home, "but I feel that I understand him better after that short talk than from all I have heard about him. Yet he never mentioned himself at all, now that I come to think of it."

He went back the next week and Brother André went to meet him. "You are not in a hurry?" he asked.

"No, I have the whole afternoon to myself."

"I have a few people I must speak to before I am free," said the Brother, "and then I will be with you."

When he came back he suggested they go to the top of the mountain. "Then we will be all by ourselves and can have a chat, alone with God and Saint Joseph."

Once up there, he pointed out all the beauties of the landscape to be seen from the summit. "It seems to me that at such a height one is nearer God," he said.

He told his visitor all about the purchase of the property and how things were going nicely with the little chapel and its additions. But when the visitor began congratulating Brother André on his success, he shook his head and stopped him. "I have had no hand in it I assure you—none at all. He is the proprietor and he and God are the only owners of this property."

They talked together for over an hour and Brother André spoke most of the time about Saint Joseph, in a loving intimate way as if he were one of his best loved relatives. When his visitor was leaving, Brother André said, "I have greatly enjoyed this hour. It is a pleasure to be free and to talk in this way after one has received a number of petitioners as I have today. What is your name?"

"Claude," said the visitor, as if he were a child at school giving his name.

Brother André laughed quietly. "Good. So I shall call you my Mr. Claude."

During the next years he proved one of Brother André's greatest allies, coming once a week at least, to see if he could help him. And in the evenings he was one of the corps of volunteers who took him in his car to visit the sick in the city.

Brother André had his Oratory now. He had a home for the Child. And he knew the Child, like Saint Joseph, did not care about storied glass windows or great bronze doors or gleaming altars. Up there on the little white altar, fashioned by the loving hands of Brother Abondius, He was content. For love had built His home and love was serving Him.

Of course there was one thing for which He had need. There ought to be a priest to say His praises and to re-enact His life daily. There must be a chaplain. It was not easy to get his service, for the priests were not numerous enough to serve the needs of a great city. And the man who came up there would have to give all his time to people who came only on pilgrimages of a few hours.

Brother André kept hoping. "Oh, Brother," he used to say to Brother Osée, "if I only had a priest here to care for the souls of the people who come to see me. They go away well disposed—but who knows if they will go to confession."

Suddenly he had his chaplain. One morning a visitor came to the Notre Dame porter. He looked up to see a young priest standing before him and rose politely. "Whom do you wish to see?" he asked.

"Brother André."

He shook his head. "I am sorry. Not here and now. Later I can see you but not during college hours. Then I shall be honoured to talk with you."

"But you don't understand, Brother. I'm not a patient. I've been sent here to be the chaplain of the Oratory. Father Dion asked me to see you and tell you."

Brother André's eyes widened. "I knew Saint Joseph would send me one soon. Come and I will ask the Superior for permission to take you to the chapel immediately, for the parlour hours are almost over."

Father Adolphe Clement drew back. His eyes were aching after a trip from the city in the sunlight and he saw rather dimly; but he could see well enough to note the look of joy which had overspread Brother André's face when he announced his reason for being there. "I must first tell you something else, Brother André. You see I have been for a brief time a professor in college. My eyes have grown very bad. I can no longer keep up with my tasks because the doctors said my sight is threatened. So I have been sent here. Perhaps," he smiled sadly, "I should not have said I was not a patient. But I have not come for help. I have come to help you—only, perhaps, not for very long."

Brother André patted his arm. "Let us leave that with Saint Joseph. He has sent you here. That is enough for me."

For weeks Father Clement fulfilled his duties and Brother André was very happy. Then one morning as they went down the road together after Mass, Father Clement said, "It is getting very hard for me to read the Mass, Brother André. I can't read my breviary at all and I can follow the Mass only because I know it so well and because the letters in the altar Missal are very large. But even they are getting indistinct now. I am afraid to try it much longer, but I have hated to tell you for I know how disappointed you will be."

Brother André walked along beside him. Father Clement, thinking he was silent from disappointment, went on talking, mostly to make him feel better. "You remember you thought I was a patient when first I came to you. Now I must tell you frankly I can't work for Saint Joseph any more unless I have my sight back."

Brother André stopped in the road, and gave the impression of not having heard this last remark of Father Clement's at all. "To-morrow you can begin the recitation of your breviary," he said to him. "Rest today, and tomorrow begin to read it before Mass."

Still sad, more because of Brother André's disappointment than because of his own unhappiness for his future, Father Clement went to his room. He picked up his beloved breviary and glanced at the pages at random. Only a blur met his eyes; only the red and black colours could be distinguished, but no letter was distinct. He put it down sadly. There was to be no help for him, as Brother André had hoped.

In the morning Brother André came up the road. Father Clement was waiting for him at the door of the Oratory. Words fell from his lips so fast he did not say them distinctly. He held out a worn breviary. "Look, Brother, I can read! I can see! When I picked it up this morning I thought I would try just once more to see if I could. I did it to please you really. I tried yesterday and it was as dim as ever, but this morning I can see. Brother André, I can read the fine words as well as the big letters."

Brother André looked at him. "But I told you to wait until this morning. Perhaps you didn't hear me say that."

"No, I didn't. But this morning when I looked once more just to please you, there it was, all the words as they used to be; not in my mind only but there on the page."

Brother André took his arm. "Of course," he said, "now you must work for Saint Joseph. Of course, he gave you your sight back when he needs you so badly here."

Together they went into the Oratory where a little group was waiting to assist at the early Mass. After it was over, one woman remarked to her companion as they went down the steep little road to the street, "What a fine voice that young priest has. I have been here before but I never heard it ring out so sure and clear. It must please Saint Joseph to have such a good voice in his service."

And Father Clement, after a thanksgiving more fervent than usual that morning, said to Brother André, as they took the road to the street: "Thanks to Saint Joseph and to you, Brother. I know now how that man in the Gospel felt when all he could say after his healing was, 'Now I see'."

CHAPTER FIVE

THE CARETAKER OF THE CRYPT

DURING 1910 and 1911 the crowds of pilgrims had grown so numerous it was obvious some more extensive building must be erected to accommodate them. In 1908 a shelter had been built : really only a big roof supported by heavy posts and set on the mountainside close to the chapel, so that the original chapel was now choir and sanctuary. That building had been made possible by a great increase in pilgrims from the United States, and there had been enough money left from the building fund to install a new heating plant, so that now the shrine was open all the year.

There had been important smaller changes, too, during these years. A bell and a belfry had been added to the chapel in 1909, and a pavilion built which included a restaurant for the comfort of the pilgrims in addition to a small office and a living room for Brother André. So after forty years as porter of Notre Dame College, Brother André was at last assigned another and a different duty. He was named caretaker of the Oratory where from then on he made his permanent headquarters.

That day in July when he left his porter's office for the last time, he made a solitary pilgrimage to his mountain. He stood and looked with joy at the Oratory which now had real windows, at the steeple with its bell, at the home which through his friends and clients he had built as a home for Saint Joseph's Son, of which Saint Joseph was the faithful guardian and Brother André, as he himself put it, "Saint Joseph's little dog."

For all the building that had been done, the mountain looked singularly untouched. The pilgrims who climbed the single road that led to the shrine found the surrounding scenery unchanged through the years. Shrubs and undergrowth still bordered the road, with vines and wild flowers everywhere; and back of them great trees hemmed the shrine.

The shrine itself looked very different from that small early structure. The entire shed which had once been built to take care of the overflow was roofed in, and made part of the church itself, so that the building no longer looked like a temporary shelter from rain and sun where people had to stand shivering with cold or exhausted from the heat.

There had been progress of another kind, too. On May 10, 1910, Archbishop Bruchési had given permission for services to be held in the chapel and had appointed a committee of three priests to investigate Brother André's manifold good works. They reported that the devotions expressed there were in every way conformable to Church tradition and practice, and it was announced that the faithful might continue visiting the shrine. The committee also paid tribute to the faith and piety of Brother André.

This meant that suspicion had now to be laid aside and forgotten, for the evidences at the shrine had been justified in no uncertain terms. Pope Pius X gave his apostolic benediction to the chapel and in November Archbishop Bruchési blessed the extension.

In 1910 a presbytery was begun but the building was not finished until 1912. It consisted of a brick structure of three stories with a stone basement. In the spring of that year an official group of Oratory workers who had hitherto been housed in the crowded college building came to take up residence on the mountain. There were three priests at the Oratory now, but the moving spirit among them was Father Clement. He was almost as constant a visitor of the Blessed Sacrament as was Brother André himself. He spent long hours in his office in the new building and sometimes this room was as filled with visitors as was Brother André's office. Beggars knew that Father Clement would be good to them, and it was to him they came—people such as the old man who occasionally climbed all the way up the mountain road to ask the priest for a pipeful of tobacco. He was a good preacher, simple and direct, with a clear, pleasant voice. Brother André's apostolate would have been less effective without this joyous priest.

In the spring of 1912 the new structure was blessed by Archbishop Bruchési. It was now so enlarged that the nave measured one hundred and forty by forty feet. Even so, hundreds who came for the ceremony had to stay outside. In the sermon preached by the archbishop there came the first indication that Church authorities were at last recognizing the fact that here on the mountain extraordinary events were taking place. The growth of the shrine, Monseigneur Bruchési said, was like that of the mustard seed of Scripture. First a pious hand put a statue there ; then prayers were offered up, then the small chapel which had been enlarged again and again.

"Shall I say miracles are wrought here? Were I to deny it I would be contradicted by these instruments and ex-votos, witness to every species of suffering. I have no need of an investigation to declare that extraordinary events are certainly taking place here. There are being wrought prodigies and bodily cures about which I admit anyone may easily be deceived. But far greater than the physical are the spiritual cures effected here.

"I strongly advise you to come here to pray," he told his audience, "and to come frequently. We can entertain no doubt as to Saint Joseph's desire to be honoured here or as to the divine blessings he obtains at this place for his faithful clients."

The archbishop said he had visited the shrine during the years and he felt only God could produce, through the mediation of Saint Joseph, such great results with such restricted means. Then he grew prophetic. "I foresee in the future that cannot be far distant, a church, a basilica worthy of Saint Joseph, rising on Mount Royal and facing the most magnificent of horizons."

Back of the altar a little man was listening eagerly. Oh, they all saw it at last—saw that his dream was not foolishness ; saw that Saint Joseph must be honoured here more and more! Brother André felt very tired in body, as a man who had been up since earliest dawn ; had been praying for hours, and had listened for a long time to the sad stories of Saint Joseph's clients. But he felt very well in spirit, as a man could not help feeling seeing his great dream come true.

That same summer came a young man, remembered as Leon, among the early morning pilgrims. He toiled slowly up the steep hillside, did not once glance at the lovely view about him or spare a look for the pilgrims kneeling along the stairway. He had his eye on one object only—the shabby building where he had been told Brother André would be. To him and him alone he wanted to tell his troubles.

"I'll come down from here cured or in my coffin," he told himself, as he put one foot painfully ahead and dragged the other after it. When he reached the little building he had to sit down to rest before he began looking for Brother André. There were already a number of pilgrims milling about, but he stood up and pushed past them as if he did not know they were there.

He was about to call aloud for Brother André, when he saw the little black figure coming down the stairs of the chapel. He went up to him without hesitation. "The doctors say my case is hopeless, that I am a doomed man. But I have come to you to hear if it is really so." He spoke in a tone of half despair.

Brother André looked at him searchingly. Then he shook

his head. "No, no, that is not true. And it is a very good thing you have come to Saint Joseph. Now come up to my room and rest a little, for I can see you are very tired."

Leon followed him to a little room, but at the doorway he stopped, for an offensive odour came to him. He traced it to one of two beds, where lay a sick man, one of his legs bound in rags through which matter was oozing. Leon drew back, but Brother André pushed him ahead as if nothing were wrong.

"Now lie down on this bed and rest quietly until I come back," he ordered. "Then I'll take care of you. This man will not trouble you at all."

When Brother André came back, hours later, he was evidently very weary himself, for there had been many pilgrims that morning. He turned his attention to the sick men and made them comfortable. Then turning out the light he left, shutting the door very quietly behind him. As if the very comfort of his presence had been enough, Leon went soundly to sleep. In the night he woke and saw his host asleep on the floor, a thin mattress under him, without blanket or sheet for covering.

Two days passed. Leon's cough was so severe he told Brother André he could not eat anything. On the third day he woke to find Brother André bending over his oil stove, cooking busily. He came to Leon's bed, his face quickened by an assuring smile. "Now here is a meal I have cooked for you myself. You are to eat every bit of it."

Leon looked aghast at the plate generously piled full of meat and vegetables. "But, Brother, I can't eat that! If all the doctors in Montreal ordered it, I would refuse."

Brother André shook his head as if gently scolding. "But of course you are going to eat it. Am I not your nurse?"

"Well," said Leon at last, "I wouldn't do it for the doctors, but since you ask me I'll try to, come what may."

To his amazement he ate the food with a relish. Even more to his amazement he did not cough at all during the afternoon. By evening he felt much better and ate with a real appetite the plate of food Brother André again brought to him. When two days later the Brother said, "Now you are well enough to go home," Leon realized he was. He had no crutch or other evidence to leave in the chapel, but he did leave there a heart full of gratitude to Brother André's powerful patron.

The Brother meantime turned his attention to the patient who was still occupying the other bed. The doctors had ordered his gangrened leg amputated ; and sometimes the man felt in such pain he thought he might as well agree to have it done ; but each time Brother André's urging decided him to wait one day more.

Later in the week, the recently healed Leon came up the mountain again, bringing an ex-voto for the chapel. With him came a friend who had long ago forsaken his Faith and for whose conversion Leon had been praying earnestly. The friend gave a sceptical glance around Brother André's little room which Leon insisted on showing him, and took one look at the gangrenous leg of the patient who was still there. The one look was enough.

"I must get away from here," he said, backing off, "or I'll be overcome by that odour. How did you ever stand it . . . here in the room with him for days?"

Leon suddenly realized that after his first entrance into the room he had not noticed the odour at all. He had not even viewed the terrible wound on the man's leg with any feeling of disgust. As they went downstairs his friend said with emphasis, "Well, if that man is cured, I shall believe again." A month later Leon called up his friend. "Now you must keep your word, for Saint Joseph has kept his. Brother André says you may come to see the man with the bad leg. He is entirely cured."

Together they again climbed the Oratory road and saw the one-time sick man ready to return to normal life again. The leg, which had been cared for by Brother André for some weeks, had shown little improvement. Then, when the cure came, it was instantaneous. The sceptic stared, and without a word went down to the chapel.

"We have brought a sinner back to his Faith," said Leon happily.

Brother André nodded. "You and I—and St. Joseph," he said.

Friends who had come in earlier years to visit often returned to the Oratory, and it was remarkable how many of them Brother André remembered, many even by name. When, in the summer of 1910, the Mivelles from Victoria came back on Corpus Christi day, he remembered them as among the first visitors to the chapel. They were waiting quietly until their turn came. They saw the Brother having trouble enough with people clutching at his sleeve and crying, "Brother André, cure me! Brother André, help me!" as he went into his office. He saw and recognized the Mivelles, inquiring if they wished to speak with him.

"Yes, we do, but not exactly in the hope of a cure, Brother," said Mr. Mivelle. "But perhaps you could make me well enough so I could again support my family."

"Go on," teased Brother André, "he's not sick, Mrs. Mivelle. He's only spleeny."

"But see how thin he is, Brother. He must be really sick," protested his wife.

"I'm thin, but I'm in good health." "Are you suffering right now?" the Brother asked abruptly, cleverly withholding a smile.

Mr. Mivelle nodded. "Oh, yes, there is continual pain." Then his expression changed to one of amazement. "No, no . . . why, the pain is gone . . . just now."

"Well, now, didn't I tell you, you were not sick!" the Brother teased. "Now go home and work like a man."

They went out in a state of dazed happiness, but stopped when they saw a weeping ten-year-old lad being carried into the office. The child's leg was terribly swollen. Brother André looked at the boy, who stopped crying, to stare at him. "Get down and walk, my lad," he said, coming close and putting his hand on the lad's arm. "You are much too big to be carried around like that."

The boy began wriggling to get down, but his father kept his hold on him and looked pleadingly at Brother André who nodded encouragement. Finally the man set the boy on his feet but continued holding him tightly until the child pulled away from his arms and began walking up to Brother André who had removed away a short distance. Then he walked back to his father, a smile on the little thin face.

The assembled pilgrims stared at the swollen leg again, but saw it was no longer out of shape or different from the other. And evidently the sensitiveness had gone too, for the boy put his foot down with assurance. There was a deep silence among the intent watchers. It was broken by Brother André's chuckle.

"Strange how everybody makes believe! They say they have this and that, and then they walk as if they haven't anything wrong with them!"

Here and there a laugh broke out, but most of the people were fascinately watching the boy, carefully and happily walking up and down the room.

Later, coming from the chapel, the Mivelles saw the boy again. He showed them how well his leg was now by climbing on a chair and jumping off. "I'm really cured," he told them. "I don't feel any pain at all"; and his eyes were shining.

The stories of cures came from the mountain, and they came from other places too; and the more spectacular were repeated over and over. There was Martin Hannon, who two years before had his legs and feet crushed in a terrible accident. When he came to Brother André he was still on crutches and had been told he must always use them. When Brother André ordered him to throw the crutches away, he did so and next day went to the newspaper *La Patrie* and told his story.

In 1911 Dr. Dufresne of Montreal wrote of the miraculous cure of his brother who had been in an advanced stage of tuberculosis. A year after the cure, the condition had been maintained, he wrote. This was the second of his patients, he added, whom Brother André had made well; the other, Alphonsine Saint Martin, had also been tubercular.

In the convent school of Saint Joseph de Levis, one of the students had a badly infected eye which had caused complete paralysis of the optic nerve. The whole school began a novena for her, at Brother André's suggestion. At the end of the novena, during the Mass, the child's voice was heard, "I can see! I can see the statue of Saint Joseph!" Two years later the sight was still good and four doctors vouched for the cure. One of them, Dr. Beaupré, said, "If the finger of God is not manifest here, I know not what finger has acted."

The change in Brother André's life when he moved to the mountain really was no change at all. He had modified his lodging and little else. His life was still the same—early and late at prayers in the chapel, busy at work to keep the church and his little office clean. His own room under the roof was larger than the porter's cell had been, but its simplicity was the same. A small oil stove, a shelf for his simple toilet supplies, a table whereon lay his few and cherished books—the *Bible*, *The Following of Christ*, the *Rules of the Congregation*, the *Prayers of Saint Gertrude*—his own hard bed, and the one a bit softer where he kept his special cases over whom he watched for a few days, or a week, or even longer.

Once a pilgrim he had lodged for the night in his spare cot sought for the Brother in the chapel when he woke. He found him sunk to the pavement, lost in prayer ; and the Brother had not even heard the pilgrim come down nor did he hear him leave the chapel again. Next morning when the visitor woke again—he saw Brother André at last coming to bed.

"How do you feel, Brother?" he asked, when later they were preparing to go to the five o'clock Mass.

"Very well." The pilgrim looked at him and marvelled. He decided that prayer was a restorative as great as sleep for Brother André.

Sometimes the priests worried about his lack of sleep. "Offer your sleep to Our Lord instead," one of them suggested. Brother André looked troubled. "Oh, you would not say that if you knew how much souls have need of me."

Of food he was as sparing as he was of sleep. Often weak farina was a whole meal for him. Breakfast he usually ignored altogether. Sometimes he slipped a few crackers into his pocket before he went to his office and then often in the evening they were still there. Or he took with him to the mountain shrine some potatoes that served as his food for the week. He complained that the food at the college was often too rich for him. His idea of a feast was bouillon with a bit of meat, pancakes made of meal, with a few vegetables and a glass of water.

New and terrifying experiences now came to Brother André more and more frequently. There had been earlier ones— temptations of the flesh when a young Brother André had showered himself with ice water or rolled in snow banks. Now came more subtle attacks, especially those of pride. In his little room he would hear a whispering : "There must be something about you to have been chosen like this. Why you? You must be a saint, André, the greatest in the country." He would close his ears. Sometimes he would argue back. "It is not my fault.

It is the good God. It is nothing of mine at all." And at length, shaken and weary, he would go to the chapel and spend the rest of the night in prayer.

Once a friend sleeping on the spare cot was awakened by a terrible noise. "Brother André," he called across to the other cot, "there must be thieves in the chapel."

"No, no," came the serene answer. "Do not be alarmed. It is really nothing to be afraid about. You should see the great black cat that is sometimes in this room when I come in alone. That is something to make you afraid. But not those noises down there. Just go to sleep." And he began praying aloud until the noises in the chapel stopped.

Once a curé made a special visit to see Brother André. Father Rector told him to go up the hill to the chapel. "It is late, but he will be up and glad to see you." The curé came back soon after, breathless. "I didn't even dare knock," he explained. "I went up the stairs but I heard the noise of scuffling and someone was saying, 'Go out! Let me go! Get out!' Are you sure there isn't someone there with him?"

"Absolutely. I know he is alone." The curé looked more alarmed than ever. "Come," said Father Rector, "we will go together and see." They found an exhausted, silent man stretched on his cot. "Satan has been here again," he said sadly. Then his eyes brightened. "And gone," he added with satisfaction.

His trips in the evenings to visit sick people were motivated by the desire to win souls to God rather than merely for physical cures. To those who accompanied him on such calls he explained that the spiritual well-being that was produced in those who invited him and in the members of their family was the really valuable result.

There was one visit of which he used to tell. "A family had requested a cure and the man they were asking it for was an unbeliever and a hardened sinner. When I came into the room I asked him very quietly, 'Do you want me to touch you with the medal of Saint Joseph? There are a great many sick people who have been cured in this way.' The bed was very low and I knelt in order to touch him with the medal. Suddenly he put both his arms around my neck and held me to him. And I said to myself, 'Ah, I have you, my lad—' And I had, too."

Even priests, among whom he lived, did not know how often he suddenly set out to call on some sick person in the city. There was no doubt, though, that his superiors knew what he was doing, as he was given a general permission to go as he liked and when he liked. After all they recognised what his errands were for and in whose name he wrought, and for whom he hurried on such errands. The individual case was not important to know about.

There were friends among the laity he could call on to take him where he wished to go in the city. Mr. Kennedy was among them, always ready to drop anything he was doing when a summons for help came. He saw many cures himself of Protestants as well as of Catholics; and he was properly indignant when two Masons who had been healed did not become converts. "Funny thing that," he said later to Brother André; but the Brother assured him that the Lord was taking care of the matter. Their part was done.

Brother André had also cured relatives of Mr. Kennedy. There was his aunt who had broken her hip. Brother André had told her to drop her crutches and walk. She did so—cured. Once Mr. Kennedy himself had very high blood pressure and the Brother had been asked for help. Overnight the patient grew much better to the amazement of his family.

All his friends had to be ready for emergency calls. One night the telephone rang in the Kennedy home. It was Brother André. "I'm calling to tell you I am going to Toronto on a train that leaves in a few hours and I want someone to talk to while I wait. Will you come down? I'm at the station now."

At the station Mr. Kennedy learned that the Brother intended going by day coach. Over his violent protests a berth was bought even while still insisting he wanted to sit up all night. Mr. Kennedy introduced him to the conductor who looked him over with great interest. "Oh, I know all about Brother André. I'll take good care of him."

Early in 1912 Mrs. Mivelle stopped off at the Oratory to tell Brother André she was on her way to the United States for a visit to Rhode Island, and that she would stop again on her way back.

"Where are you going to stay?" he asked. "I know parts of Rhode Island."

"At Natick, Brother."

"Oh, I have relatives there. Perhaps you will see them."

Mrs. Mivelle in the course of her visit, saw his relatives— two sisters and their families—and spent an evening with them.

"How proud you must be to have such a brother," she said as they sat in the parlour. "I have seen him perform the most remarkable cures." And she told them about the little boy with the injured knee and how he had jumped on and off a chair afterward to show them he was really well. Suddenly she realised they were not so enthusiastic as she was about their brother's work. In fact the sisters began to laugh, and Eugenie said, "Oh, imagine Alfred performing miracles! What next?" Mrs. Mivelle remembered that she was a guest, but she could not let such a statement go unchallenged about her cherished Brother André. "Please don't laugh. I am telling you the absolute truth. I saw the boy and talked with him and his father."

They were still amused at her evident simplicity but did not want to hurt her feelings. The other sister said, "Mrs. Mivelle, my legs are in a very bad condition from rheumatism and I can walk only with the greatest difficulty. If Alfred were to cure me I should believe your strange story."

One of the daughters who had been listening interestedly entered the conversation. "Mrs. Mivelle, I am engaged to a fine boy; the family likes him and the only reason they object to the marriage is because he is a Protestant. Do you think my Uncle Alfred could ask Saint Joseph to convert him?" Mrs. Mivelle was a bit taken aback, but she promised to speak to Brother André on her return. Then, thinking that perhaps she had been a bit too insistent about him and his powers, she said, "Perhaps he wasn't so saintly when he was younger." But his sisters both shook their heads seriously at that. And Eugenie said, "Oh, Mrs. Mivelle, you wouldn't say that if you had known him when he was a boy, or if you had seen him at the church in Farnham kneeling sometimes for hours at his prayers."

Back in Montreal Mrs. Mivelle hurried to the Oratory with her story. Brother André only smiled at her annoyance. "I am so glad you saw them all, and I am very grateful for the news you give me concerning them. You see my sisters are very incredulous and also very bashful about asking me for help of any kind. You write them that I wish very much that they would write me and tell me all these things themselves."

It was much later in the year that Mrs. Mivelle received two letters. Eugenie wrote that her legs were cured and that she walked with ease. Her sister's back, she said, was also much better. The other letter was from the niece—a letter glowing with happiness: her betrothed had come into the Church and they had been married with the blessings of the whole family. Some day she was coming to the Oratory herself to see her wonderful uncle.

In 1912 Mr. Claude, a faithful helper of Brother André in his sick visitations, decided to increase his services for his friend.

It was obvious that the man who had been a porter for so many years was now greatly in need of someone to replace him. So Mr. Claude decided to take the position. From then on he stood often in the waiting room, a tall dignified gentleman in black, and brought people to Brother André. It was no light task, for over thirty people an hour came into the little office on busy days.

Often the pilgrims saw Mr. Claude and told him their troubles first, finding him a sympathetic listener. He had only one thing to tell them all, while they were waiting to see Brother André: "Have confidence in Saint Joseph."

Another new and valuable friend came into Brother André's life at this time. He was standing in the road one morning breathing deep of the cool good air when he saw an old man plodding up. He watched him come and when the two men were abreast Brother André felt impelled to stop him. He did not even wait for a greeting. "You're just the man I need," the Brother said simply. The old man looked up and answered with equal simplicity. "Yes, I came because I was sent. I thought you needed me. I'm old but I'm strong. I will help you in any way you wish."

Later, at the presbytery, he told his story over a good breakfast. He was Joseph Malenfant, and lived some three hundred miles away in the small town of Saint-Hubert de Témiscouata. He was living alone on a farm which he had cleared from the forest years ago. He was sixty years old and felt his life was nearly over. He had reared a family, but they were all dead now except one son who had gone to seek his fortune in America. His wife had died too and he was ready to finish his last years peacefully and quietly in his small home, for he had means enough to support himself.

Instead of peace, however, he had been troubled at night with a recurring dream. He saw repeatedly an old man trying painfully to build a church, moving among unfinished carpentry, among stones piled for a foundation, kneeling before an unfinished altar. And sometimes he thought he heard the old man calling to him for help, begging him to assist him with his church.

He talked it over with his friends, but they laughed and said he was brooding too much, that he was lonely and the delusion would pass. But it did not pass, and at length Malenfant decided it must be a sign from God. He would go and see if he could find the old man who called to him. If he found no one, he would come and forget about it. He had always wanted to see Montreal, so he decided to go there first.

On his first day in the city he met a countryman, who told him he must not leave Montreal without visiting the lovely little church on Mount Royal. Malenfant set out in the trolley and reached the mountain. He looked with misgiving at the steep road before him, and began to climb the hill. On the way up he had met Brother André and recognized him immediately as the old man he had seen in his dream. This was the sign he sought.

"I told my friends," he said to Father Clement, "that there is one motto and only one which I have followed all my days. 'Not to help others is to be useless. It is better to obey God than man'."

Then he turned to the Superior, Father Dion, who had come in time to hear most of the story. "Admit me to the Community as a lay Brother, Father. I will give the rest of my life to this work, or to any work that you wish, for any work I do here will further the work of Saint Joseph."

The superior shook his head. "We know you would do any work you were asked to do, but you see you are much too old to be received into the Community. The rule forbids it and so I can be of no aid to you."

For some time Malenfant remained at the mountain, going

every day to the Oratory, praying for light as to just how he could assist in this work. Suddenly he knew at least one way in which he could help. The money that came to the shrine was used almost as fast as it came in to improve the grounds or the Oratory itself. He might be too old to be a lay Brother, but he was not too old to raise money to promote the good work of the shrine. He could cover the land, east and west, as far as his strength took him and ask for alms for the Oratory. The next morning he was gone on his self-imposed mission. He had told no one where he was going or what he proposed to do. They brought word of his departure to Brother André, who smiled and said, "He will be back."

He returned months later. He had had a good time, and a bad time too. Once a diocese refused to let him ask for alms at all, for he had no credentials. After that refusal he simply went from village to village begging for help. Sometimes he received alms, but often he was pushed aside and laughed at. To be laughed at hurt him, for he was a man well thought of in his community. He said later on : "Sometimes the devil used to whisper to me, 'You are an old fraud, and an old fool, Malenfant. You had a fine farm and livelihood, and now look at yourself : You are a tramp, a beggar, a good-for-nothing ; you sleep in barns, you tramp the highways. Go home and be sensible.' But I shook him off. I got rid of him each time by saying, 'Not to help others is to be useless.' That rid me of him—but he always came back again."

In addition to these insults he had other setbacks. He called on Father Dion and handed him fourteen hundred dollars, collected in his travels. Father Dion accepted the money in the name of the diocese, and more particularly in the name of the Oratory. Then he said seriously, "You know we value your work, and its results are excellent. I accept this large sum with great gratitude, but I want to ask you not to collect any more in this way. This vagabond life is not the way to spread the work of the Oratory. You can find better means I am sure." In anger Malenfant came stamping up the steps of the college. He spoke to the first religious he came upon. "Your Superior is not a man. He is an icicle." He turned and walked off.

Within a few days he left the city. The advice given him by the Superior, to which he felt he could never agree, had been given to him in another way by Father Clement. "Why not solicit subscriptions for our magazine, *The Annals of Saint Joseph?* You will be doing exactly the work you want, for you will be getting money for the Oratory, and best of all you will be spreading word of it everywhere. And it will bring in even more than your begging would in the end."

The idea pleased him. "I have decided to *annalise* the whole country," he punned, and departed happily. Brother André only nodded when they told him his parting remark. "He will be back," he said again.

A little later in the day his pleasure in this staunch friend was abruptly spoiled by a sudden recollection of an unpleasant duty he must perform that morning. He had promised Father Dion he would let photographers take his picture. He hated this, and nearly every picture showed a grim, stiff, unsmiling little man, very different from the pleasant one the pilgrims saw in his office or in the chapel.

Once when Father Dion has insisted, as he was doing now, on poses in two different attitudes, they showed him the finished picture and asked him which he preferred. "It's a little matter," he growled; "it's the same beast in each," and turned away. They were learning, however, to get a pleasant picture of Brother André by posing him with several other people, as they planned to do now. The others talked to him and kept him smiling, as one would to a child, while the photographers worked.

CHAPTER SIX

THE BUILDING OF ST. JOSEPH'S SHRINE

IN 1915 all Canada was shaken with the great conflict that was the beginning of the first World War. Destruction, the inevitable accomplishment of all wars, had begun. But in that same year there was being planned on Mount Royal a great stone crypt, to be built from sums contributed by pilgrims from many lands, who were making it possible to erect a great shrine for the thousands now thronging the Oratory, grown far too small for the ever increasing crowds.

While battles raged across the ocean, a contract was signed for the construction of the buildings on May 11, 1915. Permission for its erection had been given in January of the previous year. Already, however, more ambitious plans than those for the projected construction were in the offing. The crypt now to be erected would one day serve as an approach to a great basilica; and for that, too, plans were now being made by noted architects.

That year the peace of Mount Royal and the quiet of the little Oratory were shattered. Workmen were everywhere, almost as numerous it seemed as the pilgrims. Mechanical drills silenced the songs of birds. Rocks had an unpleasant way of flying through the air occasionally and falling in one's path. The little chapel was always covered with dust and its windows had to be cleaned continually. But Saint Joseph smiled through it all, as did his devoted clients.

Brother André turned sadly one day after hearing an account of what was happening to the churches of Europe—those ancient cathedrals where God had been worshipped for so many centuries. To have evil men destroy a house consecrated to God is, of course, nothing new to history. But history meant little to Brother André, nor did grandeur and greatness. It was only that he did not want God homeless or the people who came to serve Him deprived of shelter.

Brother André, loving client of the great Saint who had with his hands built a shelter for the Child entrusted to him, knew that grieving over the destruction of famous fanes because they were beautiful and rich was not grief of the spirit for injuries done to religion. He grieved because the temples of the foster Son of his patron had been destroyed, because once again He who was the world's shelter had no shelter for Himself.

He stopped to look around as he came from Mass in the early morning. Here in the new world another Home was rising. The love and faith of people were building another house in God's honour. Early as it was, pilgrims were already making their way up the stairway. Down in the street an early trolley car was emptying more of them. Some were already in the chapel when he came in and were kneeling in the pews or lighting votive candles before Saint Joseph.

When there were no pilgrims to be taken care of and talked to and cured, Brother André used to stand at the window of his small room and look at the expanse of the mountain, and dream. Once he had stood in a field in a real dream and had seen at its end a great building rising before his amazed eyes. That had been a dream that vanished with waking, but now he could feast his eyes daily on the growing realisation of his vision. At last Saint Joseph was to be properly housed on Mount Royal.

In 1916, on a beautiful day in May, the Bishop of Joliette, Monseigneur Forbes, blessed the cornerstone of the new building. One week before Christmas it was open to the public and was filled to overflowing the first day. It did not matter, evidently, how large the structure was : the loyal friends of Saint Joseph could fill it.

It was built on the northwest flank of the mountain, a little more than halfway up, a hundred feet from street level. Made of stone and reinforced concrete, it was lofty and architecturally imposing in its simple severity. Huge stones made the outer walls and sort of thick-set bastion with rounded ends. Two rows of pillars supported a great vault over thirty-five feet high. There was seating accommodation for one thousand persons, with standing room for more than twice that many. The nave was one hundred and forty feet long and over one hundred wide, and the building two hundred feet in its entire length. The central doors, with a huge candelabra of three lamps on each side, opened on a wide corridor. There were three altars in the sacristy and four side altars, so that seven Masses could be said at once.

Statues of Saint Joseph were everywhere, enough to satisfy even Brother André. On the main altar the nine-foot figure of Saint Joseph came from Italy, by special order, of the finest carrara marble, carved by a noted sculptor.

There had been a worrying delay about the delivery of this statue. The sanctuary was nearly ready and so was the main altar in white marble ; but no statue made its appearance and there was fear lest the vessel which was bringing it had been torpedoed. But on December 5 it reached Montreal and was carried up the slope of the mountain while pilgrims in the little chapel sang the *Magnificat* in thanksgiving.

The windows let in very little light, but the church was filled with the soft glow of watch lights fastened to the wall, lamps which burned for seven days for the intentions of the faithful, and in honour of the seven joys and the seven sorrows of Saint Joseph.

Of all the windows Brother André liked best the central one

behind the high altar where the patron stood holding his Son in his arms, with a background of white lilies. Candelabras of gold stood on each side of the altar and silken curtains were back of the great statue framed in a mighty golden aureole. He could not feast his eyes on all this wonder of beauty unless he came out of his hiding to see it. For back of the last stall, hidden by the altar itself, Brother André kept his vigils.

Every small side chapel had a stained glass window, depicting an incident in Saint Joseph's life : his dream, the Child's birth, the circumcision, the presentation in the temple, the flight into Egypt, the Child with the rabbis in the temple, the life at Nazareth, Saint Joseph's death. It was a lovely biography in the language of coloured glass.

Inside the central doors the wide corridors were soon covered with canes and crutches and other aids for sufferers who no longer needed them. Some, of course, were still in the little chapel which had to be moved up the mountainside now and placed at the left of the crypt. Masses were still said there, and votive lights flickered on ex-votos, although the crypt was now the appointed place for saying Mass. The old statue of Saint Joseph was set in a niche on the main altar of the little chapel. It was as it had always been, a mysterious small sanctuary of devotion.

From the platform of the crypt there was access to two stairways from which a panorama of the city could be seen. Back of the Oratory and on both sides was the primitive forest, wild and lovely ; oaks and maple, and snowy birches, with here and there a spruce or pine.

In front and closing the horizon, usually dim with fog, was the chain of the Laurentians. Far to the left of the pilgrim lay Lake Saint Louis, and beyond sparkled the waters of the St. Lawrence until they were lost in the grey horizon. Nearer the mountain was an almost level plain, with houses and fruit orchards and farm fields. Churches could be seen everywhere—over twenty on a clear day and each surmounted by its cross.

Large crowds of people had been visiting the shrine for some time. Now the crowds became so huge that the earlier ones seemed small indeed by comparison. Every day when the weather permitted, pilgrims came by thousands. The sick were sometimes carried by their friends ; or when possible dragged themselves up the long flight of steps to the crypt. Many pilgrims made the entire flight on their knees, praying at each step. And the little office where Brother André received his clients began to look, said one priest, like a confessional at Easter time.

The very early Mass at which Brother André always assisted was usually celebrated in a small chapel high in the crypt, where Father Clement liked best to say his Mass, and where Brother André was usually his server. For the two men, so busy all day long with the crowds, it was a spiritual relief to begin the day in such peace and quiet, alone with God.

Brother André loved the little lofty chapel so much that often late in the evening his last task was to climb the stairs to look in it carefully to make sure no one was lurking there. And he loved to see it in the early morning when the light of dawn had scarcely touched the mountain. Here he could best ask Saint Joseph's blessing on the pilgrims whom yesterday he had ministered to.

There were many organized pilgrims now, from schools and colleges, from workingmen come to consecrate themselves to the master workman, from school children and women's sodalities ; and often an entire parish came with a priest.

Each year on Saint Joseph's own feast day the crowds were larger than they had been the year before. Holy Mass was offered from early morning until noon and the crypt was always filled to overflowing. Often Mass was said outdoors, sometimes before the great central doors and sometimes on the roof itself. It was like a cathedral under the sky and with the sky for a vault.

One crowning cross came to Brother André during those years. On August 10, 1918, Father Dion died. Rector of the Oratory and Superior of the Congregation during his last seven years, he had been from early days the friend and aid of Brother André. He had watched the small developments of the little chapel and he had been the main builder of the great crypt. If the inspiration had been Brother André's, surely the accomplishment had been in great measure Father Dion's.

In 1920 the Catholic Association of French Canadian Youth had sent out an appeal for a pilgrimage. So many came the train service was crowded and thousands could not reach the shrine at all. Even so, there were over fifty thousand in attendance.

For one thing, it was such a pleasant place to come to. During the summer and early fall the gay dresses of the women and the red and gold of the military stood out in contrast to the black and white of priests and nuns. Pilgrims lingered long after the services were over, praying, walking about, while the Little Sisters of the Holy Family were busy with their duties in the sanctuary, and other helpers lighted the countless votive candles at the request of those who sought favours.

On the roof there were pilgrims too, looking at the panorama of grey mountains and blue water that showed the far-off lakes and the great St. Lawrence, at the city growing about the mountain's foot and distant villages settled about their spired churches. And especially they knelt often in the small old chapel to look at the ex-votos. Many of these had been placed there years before by some happy, grateful pilgrims as mute evidences of favours granted.

The little office where Brother André worked was filled

always, even when he was not there. He was so small that crowding pilgrims would sometimes think he was not there until they stood in front of him, and then they saw him, always with that asset of quiet dignity, and a smile on his lips and in his eyes.

Mr. Claude was usually somewhere about to see that Brother André was not too much bothered by the more insistent pilgrims. Before the frail little man in his shabby old habit the sick and halt passed, as he stood erect waiting for them. He took care of them all as they passed him—the girl with Saint Vitus' dance, the man with a paralysed leg, the child held in his anxious father's arms, the woman so thin she seemed a skeleton, the blind man in dark glasses led along by a friend.

Over and over he repeated his monotone of familiar words. "Rub yourself with the oil and medal of Saint Joseph. Make a novena and persevere in prayer to the saint." The person addressed passed on and the line moved slowly again. Occasionally, of course, there was the dramatic instance of an immediate cure. The number of these had grown with the years. Sometimes in silence and alone a man or woman or child was made well; or the cure was sudden and before many people in the office itself.

"Get up and walk," the Brother would sometimes say suddenly, and the paralytic walked. Sometimes there would have to be prayers and novenas. "Don't stop praying," Brother André would say with a gay light in his eyes, "or you may lose what you have gained so far," to a sick person whose cure had been only partial and who was unhappy about it. Sometimes he rubbed the sick with the oil instead of telling them to rub themselves. "My hands produce the same effect as the medal does," he explained.

Among the sick he was always calm and controlled. When he recommended prayer for the favour of a cure from an illness, he always added that it came from God who wished it for our greater good. And he added that it was not difficult for God to make us live or make us die ; and that the best way to obtain a cure was to conform to the will of God and thank Him, no matter what the outcome.

He bestowed with joy the favours which Saint Joseph obtained, but the Brother impressed the people who came to see him that they must love the suffering which had its supreme example in Our Lord Himself. "One should not always be praying for miseries to be removed," he told them, "but one should also pray for strength to bear them better." There were the saints to inspire us, all illustrating in their lives some sort of suffering, and of suffering with joy. "You see," he would encourage, "the good Lord gained some of His best friends and His greatest followers through suffering. Suffering is a thing so great and of such a high price that it can find its reward only in Heaven."

Occasionally, when he was very tired, his impatience got the better of him. "Don't bother me—go see Saint Joseph," he snapped one day at one of the Brothers who came to complain about his eyes.

"Very well," said the Brother, "I'll come back tomorrow when you are in better humour." Next day he came again and Brother André received him with a rueful smile, and rubbed his eyes gently until the pain was gone. Once a Protestant visitor thought him so rude that she left the room in tears, limping away on a leg she had hoped he would help. As she went downstairs she suddenly realized she was no longer limping.

Sometimes his irony was justified. He saw a woman stealing apples from a tree in the Oratory yard, and later in the day he recognized her among his clients. Her stomach was in a bad condition, she told him.

He looked at her coldly. "Rub yourself with the oil of Saint Joseph," he said ; then added, "don't eat any more green apples."

He expressed impatience with those visitors who said, "You must cure me, Brother." He would shrug his shoulders. "It is too bad, but I haven't the weapon." He was not pleased when people made conditions for obtaining favours ; that expressed doubt about God's mercy. "What does the good Lord owe you?" he would demand. "You cannot buy Him with silver when He does not need it."

To a girl who came to him to ask for a "gift" he said shortly, "Pray to Saint Joseph for the gift of common sense." To a man very impatient to be cured, he listened attentively. "If I'm not healed right away my leg must be amputated, the doctors say. I end my novena today and if I'm not cured I'll have it done." Brother André turned away. "As you like," he called over his shoulder. "Do you want me to send for the surgeon now?"

"They say 'Cure me, cure me'," he lamented to Father Clement. "They complain of half-granted cures. They don't seem to understand when I tell them they are not heard because they have no confidence in God. They command to be cured as if I were a doctor. I tell such people : 'If God owes you something then go and ask Him for it'."

Then his mood of anger changed to one of sadness. "I made a woman cry today," he said miserably. "Didn't you stop to think before you became angry?" asked Father Clement.

"Not a bit," said Brother André. "But I keep thinking about it later on, and I have seen that woman's tears all day." He looked so desolate that Father Clement tried to cheer him. At last Brother André's face cleared. A happy thought had come to him. "But my rages don't really matter. All that matters is that people realise it is Saint Joseph, not I, who cures them." He chuckled, happy again. "There was a lady here last week who talked and talked. I tried my best to get a word in and finally told her, 'Madame, if you don't want to listen at all, then you will have to make your own arrangements with God Himself.''

As a matter of fact, he was never half so rough with people as he thought he was. He was good to them all, but it was the lonely and the poor he loved most. It was from their stock he, like Saint Joseph, had sprung. At his office all were received with equal courtesy : poor or rich, sinners or faithful, Protestants, Jews, Catholics.

One day among his visitors was a man who said to him, "I am the chaplain to the King of England. His Majesty has read the Ham book* about you and he asked me to come to see you on my trip to Canada."

Brother André smiled politely and engaged his visitor for a few moments in conversation. Then he excused himself, saying apologetically, "There are so many sick to take care of in my office. I cannot talk to you any longer, I am sorry to say."

Most of all he hated the curious. "It is strange that people come here not knowing why they come." In contrast with those whose intentions were not high and holy there was the faith of the many who made up for the importunate sightseers. To find a pilgrim who showed perfect faith against discouraging odds gave Brother André his greatest happiness. One man who came to him had been badly hurt in a machinery accident. Brother André after looking at him searchingly said, "Go, take your crutches into the church and leave them there. Tomorrow you will be working again." The man obeyed without hesitation, but as he left the church he was limping badly and evidently in great pain. Next day he followed the instructions given him, and on his Montreal farm dragged himself behind his plough. His helper laughed at his folly ; so did his family ; but he went on doggedly through the day's work. Next morning his swollen

* *The Miracle Man of Montreal*, by George Ham.

legs were normal, the limp entirely gone. "See, that is Faith," said Brother André, his eyes happy when he heard the story.

His own life was a series of acts of faith. When he told the sick who came to him to apply the oil or medal, the request sprang from his faith. "But they must have faith, too, if they expect God to help them," he said. "The oil and the medal show interest, but it is necessary to pray to Saint Joseph, and it is necessary always and in everything to wish for the will of God."

From the United States, from South America, even from the old world, as well as from all over Canada, people streamed to see him, sick physically or mentally or morally. Many, of course, he did not heal. "I am told," he said, "when to do so." But spiritually he helped them all. Physical cures were numerous and impressive; they no longer took the trouble to keep count of them. "He mended," said one of his confrères, "as if it were a game." Yet there had to be in people themselves trust in Saint Joseph. If they had Faith, and if God wished the cure then a cure would come. "Oh, if they would all understand that it is not I but Saint Joseph that cures!" he used to sigh. And when one visitor told him that he was stronger than Saint Joseph— "for we obtain favours from you while Saint Joseph remains deaf to our pleas"—he actually fell ill and had to take to his bed for a day.

Far more than for bodily benefits, Brother André looked ever for a cure of the soul. Even when a great crowd besieged his office, he would spend an hour in the conquest of a single soul while the reception of a sick person might be over in a minute. Often he used to stop to explain carefully how temporal favours are intended to create spiritual regeneration. Cures are in a sense a means to that objective.

It was rarely that a sinner resisted Brother André when he spoke with tears in his eyes and a quaver in his voice of the

Passion of the Saviour. If dealing with a hardened sinner, he would take a crucifix from the drawer of his desk and explain the suffering of Christ, giving in detail the sorrows of each wound. He described the torn flesh, the bones broken by the nails, and told of the insults from Jews and Roman soldiers.

That was the sum of his preaching, but his words seemed directly inspired: "That which comes to him from the outside comes from above," people said. He could speak touchingly of the prodigal son, the lost sheep; he knew how to renew hope by giving examples of great sinners who had become great saints, because they expressed all their energy in loving God and God alone. "One cannot speak often enough about the divine goodness," he would say to his listeners. And as often he warned them, "It is necessary to keep ready; the good Lord said he would come like a thief in the night."

One evening he walked wearily from his office. The last woman in the procession had said to him, as she came to his desk, "I have come because I am always so very tired." He answered gently, "Then pray for me, as I will for you, for I too, am very tired."

Brother Abondius caught up with him as he was leaving, wishing to speak to him about some detail in the repair of the altar of the old chapel. "Some people," Brother André said to him, "want to tell me so many details of their ills without thinking of others who are waiting. I get impatient with them and then I am sorry afterwards. But I do think they ought to see that sometimes I get very tired."

In November, 1921, was celebrated the fiftieth anniversary of Saint Joseph as patron saint of the Universal Church. It was also the anniversary of Brother André's admission to the Congregation. At six o'clock in the morning, when it was still dark at Côte-des-Neiges, figures were toiling up the slope. The crowds increased with the hours. But when they reached the summit it was not the wide open doors of the crypt they sought first, but the shabby building at its right, where in a new habit honouring the occasion, Brother André stood waiting for them, his arms folded, a smile of deep happiness lighting up his face.

That evening soft lamps gleamed in the crypt. The organ's muted chords rolled out and incense wavered over vested priests and red robed acolytes, before the gleaming monstrance set above the tabernacle. Brother André, his eyes shining, was in his usual place back of the choir waiting for Benediction. When he heard a voice break the silence with *O Salutaris Hostia*, his cup of joy was completely filled.

CHAPTER SEVEN

THE CO-WORKER OF ST. JOSEPH

BROTHER ANDRÉ'S working day had not changed with the more imposing church or the larger throngs. It was only that now he and Saint Joseph worked harder. Otherwise, excepting for the fact that the Brother took more distant trips, often to the United States, things were much the same as they had been earlier.

When the very early Mass which he always attended was over, pilgrims were already coming up the long flight, halting a moment at the great statue of Saint Joseph which greeted them at the entrance, then slowly mounting the long avenue to the steps. The great oak doors of the crypt swung open as the first comers entered the church to hear Mass.

Brother André always went from the upstairs chapel to his own little room and ate hurriedly a few crackers and sometimes drank a little milk, then went to the office where already some visitors had assembled. This office was officially called the restaurant, for there an old woman sold candy and soft drinks to the pilgrims, as they sat on wooden benches scattered about. Brother André hurried past them as they turned at his entrance, putting out their hands to stop him or to touch his habit. Through the room went the murmur, "There is Brother André!"

He disappeared into his little office, changed his old black coat for an equally worn old habit, and was ready for his day. Usually he stood back of a table, his head bent forward a little to listen more intently. He hardly ever looked directly at the people before him. "He sees all the world without seeing anyone," said one of his friends.

He had a medal of Saint Joseph fastened to a piece of wood on the table, and while someone was talking to him, he put his hand on this medal, closed his eyes, and seemed to be meditating even while he listened.

Each day brought its same sad stories, as each day brought some joy to the afflicted. One day a woman came with her son, just at the day's end. He was studying at one of the schools of the Congregation of Holy Cross, and had been told by his family doctor he had a malignant cancer of the hand. His mother pushed him ahead of the others and explained that the boy wanted to become a priest. "Brother André, you must cure him," she pleaded.

The Brother straightened his already straight shoulders. "Come now, do you dare give orders to God?" he demanded. "You might use such language to a doctor or to me—but not to God. Go and pray in the church and learn to ask grace in a different way."

As the mother went out weeping, young Baon, her son, held back to ask a question. "May we come again tomorrow?"

"If you like," said Brother André, and turned to the last in line.

Instead of going immediately to the church the two went first to see Father Clement. He comforted the mother. "Wait till tomorrow and then go back to see him. And I'll pray for the boy, too."

So the next morning they were there again, the first in line. Brother André recognised the woman as the one whose feelings he had hurt the night before by that manner of his which he always regretted later. This time he silently rubbed the aching hand with a medal for a moment, then rubbed it with his own hand. "Don't have it amputated. It will get better," he told the mother. They went out with happy faces.

One morning a young man on two crutches stood before

Brother André's table. His legs swung uselessly. The Brother said something to him in a low voice and the young man looked at him as if he did not quite understand. He repeated the words, and the crowd saw the young man take his two crutches in one hand and try three or four timid steps without them.

"Very good," said Brother André with satisfaction, and more loudly than he had spoken before; "now go carry your crutches to Saint Joseph."

The young man, his legs trembling from weakness or fear, or perhaps both, went to the crypt dragging his crutches after him, while an awestruck crowd watched his progress. From the Brother's office to the church was a considerable distance— and he did it all alone. In the afternoon visitors saw him there, still walking with uncertain steps on the terrace, his face radiant, but holding the crutches in one hand as if afraid to give them up entirely.

In the spring of 1922 it was obvious that another church would have to be built and plans for the basilica were again considered. The growth since 1905 had been phenomenal. Then it had been small groups who came to join Brother André in prayer or individually to see him for help of body or mind. Long ago they had grown too numerous for the little chapel, in addition to Mr. Sauvage's store and the tramway station. Now they were too many for the great crypt.

In the early days donations had been modest. They were still individually so, but groups had grown to multitudes, so that by 1922, with no resources except voluntary offerings and with no advertising, over seven hundred thousand dollars had been expended in clearing and building.

The Confraternity of Saint Joseph now numbered eighteen thousand. The little magazine, *The Annals*, had sixty thousand subscribers. Over eighty thousand letters a year came from all over the world, and it took four secretaries to handle the correspondence of a lay Brother who could scarcely read the letters or answer them with his pen. Of the letters, nearly seven hundred a month were thanksgiving for favours received.

Now with a public subscription authorised by the archbishop, plans were begun for the building of a basilica, the minimum cost of which was set at three million dollars. It was to be over three hundred feet long and over two hundred wide. It was to have a huge dome ninety feet in diameter. The mammoth project pleased Brother André greatly, since to him it meant three fulfilments : more honour for his patron, more shelter for the pilgrims, more space for Masses, confessionals and priests. The devotion to Saint Joseph on Mount Royal was growing and growing. This was the chief thought of Brother André when he had time from his duties to think about it at all. Monseigneur Gauthier of Montreal expressed the same thought in this way : "Monseigneur Bourget's prayer is granted. Saint Joseph has his sanctuary. Devotion to him is spreading and being intensified from day to day."

For one thing the Oratory was so situated that it was easy of access. It was located in the very metropolis of Canada and in a location almost entirely Catholic. Some great shrines are in small isolated spots, but this one was in the very centre of the nation. So great was its attraction that some days—especially those devoted to Saint Joseph—the number rose as high as five thousand, and on days of special pilgrimage there were twice that number.

Now, in the spring of 1922, the drilling and blasting began again. It took three whole years to complete the digging, and the great pile of rock was heaped at one side to be used as a base for terraces in front of the shrine. Only when everything was ready for the foundation of the colossal edifice would the building begin.

In 1924 the Guardians of the Shrine decided it was time to bless the cornerstone of the future building, for that year was the three hundredth anniversary of the selection of Saint Joseph as patron of Canada. With the Apostolic Delegate, Monseigneur Di Maria presiding, and with over thirty thousand pilgrims assisting, the cornerstone was laid—a block of granite which was later placed in a kiosk close to the crypt until it could be cemented into the future church.

While the pilgrims were gathered about after the ceremony in lovely May weather a stir in one part of the crowd drew the attention of all.

"I'm cured! I'm cured!" they heard an excited woman's voice calling.

"A miracle! A miracle!" the words swept through the assemblage.

Only later did most of the pilgrims learn the story from twenty-one-year-old Marie Doyon herself. For two years she walked on crutches because of an injured knee, and the doctors told her she would always limp and need a crutch. The Sunday before Father Theoret had applied a medal to her knee, but there had been no improvement or cure. Two days later she climbed the stairs but with great difficulty, and Father Clement, seeing her, had taken her to Brother André after the celebration.

"Drop your crutches, child," he said to her. Without hesitation she let them clatter to the floor. Now she was telling her story to the crowd. She was walking up and down, as the people pressed forward so close she could hardly take a step forward. She was saying exultantly over and over, "See, how I can walk! And now I can even genuflect!"

Back of the altar Brother André was accustomed to watch ceremonies and great throngs with shining eyes. He always stole away to some hiding place when a great religious function was in progress. But this time he had to stay to see how Saint

Joseph was honoured and to watch the ceremonies and the assembled. In honour of the occasion he was wearing a new habit. He hated to put on new clothes. Years before when he was still a porter at the college, he asked a student one day whether his mother could perhaps make one new habit out of two old ones. The mother, happy to be asked to do it, came to get them, then shook her head over the condition of the leftovers. "I can perhaps find you other old ones to make over if these prove too bad, and I'm afraid they will." Later when she brought him her workmanship, "Ah, you did manage. I recognise some bits of the old habit."

He often made his own slippers, shirts and pantaloons. Even now one would sometimes find him mending his clothes. These latter he hoarded ; and for another reason than economy nowadays. He grew extremely annoyed when he was asked for something of his as a keepsake.

"One guards the relics of the saints—not of people like me," he told petitioners ; and refused peremptorily to give them anything. When he heard that some of his own religious were saving his old garments he began carefully counting out every bit of laundry, and complaining vigorously if anything was missing. When his habits grew too old for mending or wearing, he began in his later years to burn them in the furnace and waited until they were completely ashes before he left them.

The new building would have to proceed very slowly as everyone knew. Even with the many donations and with the promise of more to come, the amount it would cost was a staggering sum to contemplate. The planned measurements were three hundred and forty feet in length, two hundred and forty in width, and three hundred and sixteen feet in height. The necessary funds for such an edifice would have to be collected over the years, since all the money was to be realised from the thanksgiving offerings and gifts from Saint Joseph's friends. Some of these offerings might be large but most of the donations would be the modest gifts of the poor.

When Brother André went now to see how the structure for his patron progressed, he saw only an accumulation of scaffoldings, a great mass of machinery and stones. It was a far different sight from the scene on almost the same spot some twenty years before, when Brother André had directed a few workmen in building a little chapel with no windows and a narrow road by which pilgrims might come up the hill. Then the skilled hands of Brother Abondius had been enough to erect the altar.

He stood there one day with some of the priests from the college who came with him to see the progress made. They appeared a little dubious when they saw how little had been accomplished and how much was yet to be done. Not so Brother André. He shook his head at them in gentle reproof, and said with the confidence of one who is sure. "It is going to be a success. Saint Joseph's basilica will be completed."

His great regret, the saddening thought in all this project, was that Father Dion was no longer there to help. That zealous priest had put all his energy and all his talent into the building of the chapel and the crypt, and by a strange irony Father Dion's funeral sermon was the first to be preached there. And Brother André had echoed, kneeling in sadness back of the altar, the words of Monseigneur Bruchési, who preached the eulogy : "To him we owe in great part this temple. The happiest person present at the dedication of this crypt was Father Dion himself."

Through the following years the work of building went on. So many had been anxious to see how the future basilica would look that the architects had constructed a small model of it and placed it on view in the kiosk where the cornerstone was placed. A card stated what the size of the building would be in actual feet. It would seat five thousand persons. It would be one hundred and fifty feet above street level. The structure seemed so colossal it sometimes appeared the work would never be finished.

From the beginning the building had been dependent on voluntary and unsolicited funds. Hence the work sometimes went ahead rapidly, sometimes almost stopped entirely. Contributions determined speed. But fast or slow, for some years the basilica was only a huge mass of scaffolding, machinery and stones of various sizes. To some eyes it seemed a vain hope that this unwieldy mass should ever grow into the beautiful structure promised by the little model in the kiosk.

But Brother André's eyes never held such a look nor did his heart ever despair about the ultimate result. Every day and every year he was serenely sure. His own work went on unceasingly—the daily toil, prayers, the crowds of pilgrims, the visits—more and more extended—over Canada and the United States. And funds continued to come in—for Saint Joseph. Always his eyes were bright with certainty, his heart sang with hope, Saint Joseph's clients would be housed better, and the more clients the more the house would grow to hold them.

By 1926 his dream had almost become a fact. The edifice stood out white against the grey background of eminence: a hill of granite on a granite mountain. The stone used in the building was native Canadian with a marble finish that held bits of rose and green and blue. The huge pillars were grouped in three columns, each one supporting the stone statue of an apostle. The crypt was dwarfed now by this giant which stood above it.

In that year there was another long halt in the work due to lack of funds. Those who had looked at the mass of stones and said the walls were never going to go up, continued pessimistic. They asserted there would never be enough money to put the roof on the great dome. But Brother André continued to pray and hope.

November 19, 1929, was the twenty-fifth anniversary of the foundation of the Oratory. The name which Brother André had given it was still used for the great crypt, for the charm and the character of the small chapel were still there on the mountain. It was still a house of prayer where every visitor felt a closer intimacy with God. There were not a few though, who called it the Oratory of Brother André instead of by its correct title, the Oratory of Saint Joseph. After all, there was a certain correctness in calling it that, for Brother André was the builder.

On that long day in 1904 a handful of people had gone up the narrow path to place a statue of Saint Joseph on the home-made altar of a windowless little building. Now up a wide avenue bordered with green came Cardinal Rouleau, archbishop of Quebec, to celebrate a pontifical Mass. Five bishops were present and hundreds of priests and religious, as well as thousands of pilgrims. There were many of the religious there who had taken part in the ceremony of twenty-five years before. Perhaps the most impressive Mass was that celebrated by Father Geoffrian, the priest who had said the first Mass in the early chapel. He was ninety-one years old, and he was attended by an eighty-year-old altar boy—Brother André himself. The Brother, instead of looking his age, wore a flush of youth on his wrinkled face. His movements around the altar were as quick as a boy's that day, though his pace with the years had become a slow, shuffling gait. Another famous altar boy of the day was Brother Abondius, who served Mass in the same little chapel, so much of which had been the work of his hands, and at the altar which he had himself built. It was a wonderful day for all the workers at the shrine and for all who had helped, whether in large way or small, to erect the towering structure that stood so close to its tiny forbear.

Late in the evening, when everyone had gone home, and when Brother André had at last been able to leave the pilgrims

milling about him to go to his own small room, the mighty
building was entirely empty of people. The flicker of lights
was the only illumination—the small twinkling vigil lights and
the taller wall lamps.

When Brother André was sure everyone had gone, he crept
back into the church until he came to the niche which held
hundreds of crutches and ex-votos. The lights from the vigils
were reflected in a pair of steel spectacles. He noted a pair of
shoes there, one of them heavily padded to make it higher.
He sat in a pew for a little while instead of kneeling, for it
had been a hard day. He was trying to remember about those
shoes, which had evidently been very recently added to the
collection. Then he smiled, for he remembered the young man
who had dragged himself so wearily into his office that morning
and gone out as wearily. But he must have done what Brother
André had told him to do—come to the crypt and prayed.
And he must have gone away again in the pair of ordinary
shoes which his mother had so hopefully carried with her when
they came together to Brother André. So he had gone away
not limping, but straight as the soldier he had once been ; and
he had confided to Brother André he hoped to be a soldier
again, if only Saint Joseph would help him.

Brother André picked up from the pew beside him a thick
cane and crutches, their cloth-covered tops shiny and frayed
from years of use, which he had brought with him. He laid
the cane carefully along the foot of the pile and looked for a
place to hang the crutches with the others. So many were there
that it was getting hard to find room for more. The cane? That
had belonged to the man who had spent the night before on
the spare cot in Brother André's room. And the woman to
whom the crutches belonged had come to say good-bye in the
afternoon, her face shining with hope and joy. She must hurry
home and tell the children, she said. Not until they actually

saw her and she saw their faces as they looked at her walking, could she believe it was really true. He found a place for the crutches and then he knelt down to pray. He rested his head in his hands wearily on the back of the pew in front of him. Sometimes, after a heavy day like this, he began to feel the years. He knelt for a long time in prayer. His heart was thanking God for His great mercies—for the crypt in which he knelt, for the magnificence of the ceremonies in honour of Saint Joseph, for the cures of the man with the cane and the woman with the crutches.

That woman whom he named here last in his prayers—he sighed when he thought of her. He had been impatient with her—and on such a day. She had come to him just as he was ready to go away for a little rest and she all but insisted he cure her on the spot.

"I'm no doctor. Saint Joseph cures," he told her and nudged her towards the church. "Go there and pray to him instead."

Later she hunted him up to tell him the rest of her story. She had gone almost in anger and certainly without hope. But as she went sadly up the steps of the crypt she felt something stirring in her. She caught her crutches closer to her and then realised that she had been standing erect on the steps and that she was not using her crutches at all. She took them in one hand with the other held the railing along the stairs until she reached the top. Then she remembered and went to pray in the church, and later hurried to tell him her story.

"You see I prayed before you did," he laughed, the weariness gone from his face in his joy. "You were insistent—but I should have remembered it was faith that made you insistent. Give me the crutches. You won't need them any more."

He was very happy, for he had not been certain of her cure before she left his office. Then he knew. "But how do you know?" they often asked him, even those in authority, and he always felt at a loss, for he could not tell how he knew. All he did know was that when he confronted a group of sick people he felt assured who among them would be cured. And when people insisted on knowing more he had only one answer. "I am told," he would say simply.

Sometimes even those whose loved ones he had once cured did not understand why he could not cure again in another emergency. There was Captain Murphy, the retired police captain, who had been his close friend for years and had gone with him on visits to the sick and had seen many a miracle performed. Long ago Brother André had cured Mrs. Murphy of what the doctors had diagnosed as cancer of the face. He was very fond of the Murphys and the captain had more than once stayed out so late with Brother André on his visits of mercy that instead of going home he spent the night on the spare cot in the chapel.

"But you must telephone first and see if your wife minds," Brother André always cautioned him.

Now, ten years after that cure, the captain's wife had died of heart trouble. Captain Murphy in his grief said to Brother André, "You say you are such a friend and you didn't help me. My wife is dead."

Brother André looked very unhappy. "But one cannot go against the will of God," he said, and there was anguish in his voice.

His prayers over, Brother André looked around the crypt. It was very late and he knew he ought to be in his own room resting in his bed. But on great occasions like this one he liked to sit here sometimes when everyone was gone and remember some of the miracles Saint Joseph had procured for him. He thought now of them an who had come all the way from Orange in the state of New York, and told him how years before when he was a little lad Brother André had helped rid him of a terrible ear-ache.

"And can I do something for you now?" asked Brother André. But there was really no need to ask. The crutches, the bent back, the sagging knees told the story of the paralysis that was affecting even his head muscles. Brother André examined him carefully and told him to sit down and rest a bit.

"They want to operate on me, Brother," he said and looked at him fearfully, "and I am afraid that will be the end."

Brother André stood silently before him for a few moments, then patted the man on the sholder. "No operations for you," he said briskly. "But go for a visit to the church and come back later." The man reached for his crutches but Brother André stopped him. "Never mind them—just leave them here till you come back."

He hobbled out and over to the church. He stayed close to the wall in case he grew too weak and felt himself falling. But there was no need of such precaution, for he was really walking. He told Brother André later that he kept glancing around, for it seemed strange that no one noticed he was walking when the act expressed so wonderful a miracle. When he came back from the church he found Brother André smiling jovially. "Take the crutches with you," he told him. "Use them now and then when you get tired, but you won't need them long."

And there was the little girl whose father brought her to Brother André holding her in his arms, the wasted little legs dangling uselessly in the air. He held her out silently, and as silently Brother André felt the legs, and patted her head and smiled at her. Then he waved the father to go away, and the latter's face grew even sadder, for he thought he was being dismissed. He had come so far and had been so full of faith and hope. Evidently God was not going to help his little girl. But, on coming to the outer door of the office, the little girl stirred

in his arms. She wriggled to get down, and he held her more
closely for fear she would fall. "Put me down, Daddy, put me
down," she said shrilly. "I want to walk by myself." In alarm
the father looked at Brother André as if to share his sadness
with the kind old man. He saw to his amazement that the
Brother was nodding his head, "Yes, put her down. She'll be
all right."

Fearfully the father set the child on her useless legs. The
legs remained firm on the floor, and after clutching at his hands
a few times, she began to walk, a step or two at a time, then
a little faster, until she reached Brother André and he opened
his arms to her and hugged her. "Now," he said, "walk like
that to your father." He still remembered the look of love and
joy on the man's face as he held out his arms.

Brother André remembered, too, the time when men of
science began to take a real interest in his cures and the cry of
"charlatan" was no longer heard so loudly. He could remember
now, miracles attested to by physicians. In fact his memory was
still so excellent he could remember even the dates of some of
the miracles. There was one remote cure, a case of advanced
tuberculosis, that of a man named Dufresne who came back
eleven years later to visit Brother André and to tell him he was
still cured. And he told him, too, that his doctor, who had
believed his death imminent, had admitted after a year that the
cure was permanent, and was still admitting it. That had been
in 1911, the same year that young Veilleux had come to him in
a plaster cast, the victim of tuberculosis of the spine. Three
weeks later he went home without the cast and with no trace of
the disease, so said his doctor when he reached there. And also
that year (there had been many cures in 1911; it had been a
busy year for Saint Joseph and a successful one), the Breton
woman with a cancer of the right arm in the malignant stage,
had been cured. He remembered well the doctor's report of

her case which she sent him : "Ganglions disappeared and no trace of the disease left." The year before, L'Heureux of Quebec was cured of hip trouble—an instant cure—and a cure that was permanent. He came back for a visit some years later. "I carry myself very well today," he said proudly, "just as I did the day I was cured."

Two years ago Mrs. Marcoux was dying of heart disease in her home in Quebec. The doctor said her case was hopeless and her death a matter of weeks. That month Brother André was visiting at the Holy Cross house in Quebec and the woman's husband had come to him and told the story. The Brother had sent him away a little later, and that evening he had come bursting in again to tell Brother André excitedly that when he got home his wife was sitting up—dressed, waiting to tell him how she had suddenly, a few hours before, felt entirely well. A little later her doctor certified to the cure.

There was the man who told of his sister's cancer of the breast. "Three sides decayed," he told Brother André, "and an immediate operation is all that can give even temporary help." Brother André knew that he could help her only if she had faith. "Tell her not to be operated on. Saint Joseph will cure her." For several afternoons the man came back and the burden of his talk was that his sister was worse—that she was going to die. "If it is the same sickness she will not die," said Brother André firmly. The sick woman listened to what she was told and had followed Brother André's advice faithfully in prayer and hope. Before the week was over the cancer had disappeared and she was well.

One of the loveliest of his memories was one of unselfishness in a client. A girl came to see him with the story of a very sick sister. "If you could only help her, Brother!" she pleaded.

He looked closely at her. "But why not ask health for yourself, child?"

She shook her head. "No, it's for my sister that I have come. I can manage for myself."

But for her faith and her love Brother André was able to cure her of a very bad heart condition, much worse than her sister's illness, and promised aid for the latter, too.

Brother André shook himself. It was time to stop all this and go to bed. But as he rose he thought suddenly of one more client—the Protestant, Mr. Standhope, whom only the other day he had watched climbing so painfully up the Oratory steps. His leg had been broken in a fall, he said. It was healed now, but there was a great wound on the leg which refused to heal. When Brother André put his hand on the wound, the sick man said it ached very much less. In a few minutes the suppuration stopped and before the day was over the sore was entirely well.

As he left the pew and went slowly through the dark he was thinking of those children still outside the Faith, and he wished they could heed the call of God and enter His house after such signal favours. He said a last little prayer for Mr. Standhope and the other sheep outside the Fold.

CHAPTER EIGHT

BROTHER ANDRÉ VISITS THE UNITED STATES

DURING the later years of his long life Brother André did a great deal of travelling; not for his own pleasure, however, for travel as such meant little to him. Even the radio he admitted only grudgingly to have at least one value: it was excellent for transmitting sermons. He loved speed when he was in an auotomobile and often asked his driver to go faster.

By train and by car he covered a good share of the United States and of many parts of Canada. As a rule the visits were mainly connected in some way with Saint Joseph and funds for his work. Occasionally he went for another reason. There was Dr. Mahoney in Springfield, Massachusetts, who had years before taken care of him in some surgical work. Brother André was already ready to listen to physicians and follow their advice, if once the authorities insisted he see a doctor. Years before Dr. Mahoney had cared for him, and now Brother André heard that the physician was very ill himself, and he made the long trip from Canada, just to see him and give him what consolation he could.

He loved California and had many friends there. One of his first cures in the United States took place in Pasadena—that of a young man whose doctor had given him up, saying he had an incurable form of influenza. Friends asked Brother André to see the young man and he agreed. He touched him with a medal and prayed over him. Many years later he saw him again, hale and hearty.

In the various towns he visited, people who had heard of the healer from Montreal gathered about him and were amazed to see what he really looked like—a shrewd-faced little man, with an air of youth about him in spite of his grey hair. People whispered that he talked right to Saint Joseph, and some added that he was a saint himself and did his own miracles. When news of that came to him he resented it and looked sad. "But it is not true," he repeated patiently each time he heard it. "It is not I who heal but Saint Joseph." Often in his travels he met again people who had come to see him at the Oratory. In 1921 he stayed at the home of the Mivelles, who had often crossed his path, notably when he cured Mr. Mivelle and later, indirectly, when Mrs. Mivelle met the Brother's relatives.

By that time, of course, he was well-known throughout all Canada, and when news spread through the town of Victoria that Brother André was coming, a crowd of people began to gather around the Mivelle home, among them a great many who were ill. On his arrival he accepted the situation as calmly as if he were in his office on Mount Royal, and asked that the people form in a procession and file past him. The familiar words, "Pray fervently to Saint Joseph. Rub yourself with the medal," were repeated over and over, until, after some hours the Mivelles became worried about their guest's endurance.

After supper, in order that Brother André might have a respite from clients, the Mivelles took him to meet the parish priest of the town, Monsignor Milot. The monsignor was polite enough but eyed the little man somewhat critically, for he was among those of the clergy who did not put much stock in Brother André and his cures.

"One of our own workers here has been very ill. She has been confined to her bed for the past six weeks with inflammatory rheumatism," Monsignor said tentatively.

Brother André looked up, as he always did when the sick were mentioned. "Will you come with me so that I may see her?" he said. The monsignor took him to the patient, followed

by a curate and the Mivelles. Brother André stood by the bed
and looked at the patient whose pain-racked face stared up at
him from the pillow. He did not even smile this time. "Get
up," he said. It was a command. Miss Poithier sat up immediately, then moved slowly until she was sidewise on her bed.
The visitors saw that her legs were enormously swollen.

Her eyes fixed on Brother André, she put one foot on the
floor and then the other. She looked with alarm at the badly
swollen limbs. Then she looked up at the Brother again, as if
for encouragement. His face was non-committal. He merely
continued watching her. Suddenly she made up her mind,
stood on her feet, took one step forward, then another. Her
face alight with excitement, she called out, "My knee bends!
My knee bends!"

They left her still moving about on the legs from which all
pain had gone. And at last Brother André, after watching the
knees bending naturally, gave her a smile and his usual advice
about praying to Saint Joseph. Later, when the guests were
leaving, he and Monsignor Milot looked at each other for a
long moment. Then Monsignor smiled. "Thank you, Brother,"
he said gently. Brother André smiled too. Then, with like
gentleness he said, "No, no, Father, no thanks are due me. It
is Saint Joseph. He can do anything."

"But tell me one thing, Brother? How do you make these
decisions without hesitating at all?" the priest asked.

There was the usual brief delay in answering when this
question was asked. He looked at Monsignor Milot in silence
as if he wanted to phrase his answer carefully for the priest.
"You see, very often, it is evident that they will be cured,"
he answered simply.

When the Mivelles brought their guest home, to theirs and
his own astonishment a crowd of people was waiting for him.
Once again the line formed and the procession passed before

him. The village bells rang midnight and it was long after that before his hosts and their guests were again alone.

They hoped to let the tired little Brother sleep late the next morning and planned to keep the house very quiet. But he was up again before five, ready to assist at a five-thirty Mass in the village. No matter where he was, he insisted on receiving Communion before he did anything else. If he came later in the day, there was always a request to be taken to the church for a visit to the Blessed Sacrament and a second request— that his host or the chauffeur return for him in one hour. There was one favourite prayer which he always said, and he suggested it to his friends, asking that they add it to their other orisons : "Oh, Holy Angels, fill me with love for Our Lord on the altar, as you are filled with the love of God in heaven."

In 1934, when Brother André was travelling through New York, his car met with tyre trouble and had to be taken to the Millette garage for repairs. Mrs. Millette entertained the Brother at lunch and heard for the first time the story of the Shrine and its cures. The following year the Millettes visited Montreal, anxious to see Brother André again. He had invited them to come and they had assured him they would do so. They went to the early Mass and saw him kneeling far back by the main altar of the crypt. They had intended speaking to him at the end of Mass ; instead they found themselves assisting at two more Masses, and Brother André was still kneeling in the spot where they had seen him at six o'clock. So they gave up the interview for the time being and went to breakfast.

Wherever he went during these later years, crowds formed around him, for his fame had spread. At first this was especially true of Canada where he was first known and where a very strong Catholic element predominated. But in the United States too, as time went on, he found demonstrations in his honour, though he in his simplicity was usually unaware that they were meant for him. Once, when he came to Jersey City, a party had been arranged quite spontaneously in his honour: a procession in which most of the parish participated. When he reached home, he said to the rector, "I came to Jersey City just as the parish was celebrating some great feast. It was very enjoyable to me, too."

He seldom realised that things were done especially for him. Once when he missed his train in Ontario the stationmaster arranged to have the next train stop for him and transfer him to Toronto in a fast express which also made a special stop for him in response to orders sent ahead. Back at the Oratory, unaware that anything unusual had taken place, he spoke glowingly of the kindness of the stationmaster and the facilities of the road. "There is a man who knows how to deal well with travellers!" he said proudly.

At Ottawa, visiting one day at the home of a friend, the casual count of the people assembled to see him, mounted to at least fourteen hundred. And one afternoon in Montreal, in the Rue Bienville, his car was surrounded by a great crowd of the sick and lame and by people who had brought their children for his blessing. Yet word that he would be there had gone out only fifteen minutes before. Those in the car with him that day said later that they had all had the same thought as they viewed the scene. They thought of Our Lord and of the time when it was chronicled that multitudes rushed out to see Him, wanting only to touch His garments "for virtue went out from Him and healed all."

The coachment in the early days, and later the chauffeurs, often had their hands full at such times. Sometimes they had to ask for help to disengage the crowds so that the vehicle could go on. Brother André used to remind them of the story of Don Bosco and his coachman. "He grumbled that he would rather take the devil out than a saint. . . . I'm not a saint nor

the devil, but I seem to be as much trouble as either of them,"
he said laughing; and they laughed too.

At the home of M. Laurent he received well over a thousand
people in one afternoon and hardly had time to talk to his
hosts or to eat. But he took home from that brief visit three
pairs of crutches to add to the great pile in the crypt.

Another of the friends who aided him in his visits to the sick
and in his travels was Conrad Laporte, who came with his wife
to see him for the first time in 1919. Mr. Laporte suffered from
an asthmatic condition due to gas poisoning during the war.
Brother André prayed with him and massaged his chest until
he felt much better. There was no cure asked for or expected,
but always through the years there was some help. In later
years he often travelled with Mr. Laporte as his companion—to
Quebec, to Toronto, and to other cities, where there were
always thousands to see him and ask for his prayers, and where
he often had need of someone who saw that he did not overdo.

They often shared a stateroom, for Brother André always
refused to take one for himself alone though Mr. Laporte would
urge this; and then they prayed together in seclusion. Once
when prayers had gone on for a very long time, Mr. Laporte
turned to Brother André and asked mildly, "Brother, are you
intending to pray all night?"

"You go to bed and sleep," said Brother André by way of
answer. "You must be very tired. I'll turn in later." But when
the other man woke up after a considerable sleep, there was
Brother André—still on his knees, erect and wide awake in the
swaying train. Mr. Laporte fell asleep again and woke in the
morning to find Brother André shaving. To his horror he saw
it was an old-time razor, which the Brother was busily plying
as the train swayed while travelling at great speed.

"Heavens, Brother!" he called, "you will cut yourself with
that primitive thing, without even a mirror to guide you."

Brother André looked over and laughed. "I never cut myself and I don't need a mirror." Later he laughed again when he saw Mr. Laporte, a man only half his age, using a safety razor and a mirror, too.

Whenever he was at home in Montreal during his later years he was in the habit of dining every week with the Laportes. He ate little, preferring dry bread and strong coffee, but he was usually persuaded to add to that a cup of chicken broth, or a bit of beef fillet and a potato. But they always kept dry bread on hand for him, and there was always plenty of coffee.

When Brother André came to the United States a favourite stopping place was at Keeseville, New York. The rector of the church there, Father Cornish, said in later years that he learned more from Brother André in a spiritual way than from all the priests he knew put together. He often told the story of Brother André's first visit to him.

They had gone together to the parish house by motor and then parked at the foot of the street, for the church and the rectory were on a hill above the town. Brother André was chatting away about his wonderful journey on the train and how good everyone had been to him, when suddenly he stopped. "What time will you have devotions in the church tonight?" he asked.

"What devotions?" asked Father Cornish, bewildered at the sudden question.

"Aren't you going to have devotions in the church tonight at all?" Brother asked in surprise.

"But this is a weekday, Brother. We never have anything special on weekdays."

Brother André looked down into the valley at the houses set at the mountain's foot. "Look, every house is lighted with at least one light," he said. "It seems too bad not to light up God's house, too. The people down there go to each other's houses and talk in the evenings sometimes I am sure. Don't you think they would come up here to visit God's house if you had it lighted?"

Father Cornish hesitated before this simple question. "Well, we do have a Holy Hour every first Thursday," he said.

Brother André shook his head. "That is good, but I think God would like one every week better."

"Oh, Brother, the people would never come that often. We have all we can do to get them up on Sundays and holydays. I couldn't light the church up and have no people come and be laughed at for my pains."

The smile faded from Brother André's face, and he looked very determined and very serious. "Listen to me, Father. I won't go a step farther until you promise me you will have a weekly Holy Hour for your people in a lighted house of God."

Father Cornish brought up various arguments against any such attempt, but Brother André finally won his promise and went on happily up the hill to the rectory. He stayed for one of the promised Holy Hours and had the pleasure of seeing a considerable group—drawn no doubt by the news that the famous Brother was there. Brother André insisted he knew better—they had come to honour the Lord in His house.

But when he came back to visit the next year, Father Cornish acknowledged how right Brother André had been. "The crowd you saw was doubled the next week," he told him, "and before long people began coming from neighbouring parishes which had no Hour, and now our church is packed each time. How did you know it would work like that?"

Brother André smiled but said nothing.

CHAPTER NINE

"ARISE AND WALK"

YEARS before Brother André had assured Archbishop Bruchési
that there was no direct supernatural influence in his work.
He meant that, of course, and believed it because his humility
was so deep. But more and more the evidences of such influence
accumulated through the years. And the people who came to
him had their first faith of all in him, to his own distress. Once
a letter came to him addressed, "To the Brother who works
miracles."

He said so little about himself and was so secretive that only
now and then came direct evidences. There was of course the
long ago vision which Saint Joseph had showed him at the
rectory at Farnham : the great building suddenly coming to
his view at the end of the long row he was hoeing. Every day
he could see and enter such a building now. There was the
day when he said in the midst of a conversation, "Saint Frances
of Rome has well advised me—" and then broke off and would
say no more.

In the fall of 1931 he had a vision about which he told
Father Adolphe Clement the next day. "I was on my cot and
it was late, very late last evening. Suddenly there was before
me a luminous image and it was shaped like a heart. Oh,
Father, I truly felt I was in Our Lord's presence. I felt Him
all about me. But, of course," he added with his great regard
for truth, "I did not see it distinctly enough to swear to it."

He told Father Clement that it had faded slowly away, while
he strained his eyes to keep it in sight. And, as the warm glow
was still in the room, he saw—"and this very distinctly, Father

—Our Lady and she held her Baby in her arms. I managed to get up from my cot. I wanted to be respectful and kneel and all I could say was 'My Mother, oh, my Mother, my good Mother.' And I kept on saying that until they faded away with the heart . . . and it was dark again." His own eyes were dark with the wonder and the mystery of that vision.

One day in the little shrine where candles still glowed for those who wished to pass some time there, Adelhard Fabre, one of the workmen, had gone in after work to say a prayer. The church was very dark but he could see the still figure of Brother André close to the altar in the centre of the building. When he looked up from his prayer he was amazed to see the statue of Saint Joseph shining in the darkness and, as it were, coming forward on a luminous cloud. In his amazement and fear he called aloud, "Brother, Brother!" But the silent figure in front of him did not move or answer him. The workman ran out of the chapel, pale and shaken. Brother Abondius was putting his tools away and he stammered his story to him.

"Come, tell it to Father Rector," suggested Brother Abondius to the worker, and they went to the college and told their story. The men there did not attach much importance to the narrative. "Are you sure you did not fall asleep?" Fabre was asked. He shook his head vehemently. "No, I was not sleeping. And I am in excellent health. That apparition lasted a good three minutes. I could never be so upset by a dream or by imagining something." When Father Rector asked Brother André about it later, all he had to say was, "I saw nothing, Father, nothing at all. I was praying."

Sometimes the people who followed him as he was making the stations were sure they saw a light—a sort of fire shaped like a star—on his head as he went from one to the other. Sometimes people said they felt someone going along beside him as they also followed him. And once several of the religious, coming to bring Brother André from his stall back of the altar where he had remained to pray when the rest left, saw that part of the choir filled with a strange clear light—"alive" they called it. But Brother André was apparently unaware that anything unusual was happening. He was praying, his eyes tightly closed, as was his wont.

Brother André had no learning but he had wisdom, a wisdom which God Himself had put in his soul, and there was no necessity to learn much more from books. He knew that to hear the voice of God it was necessary to silence in oneself the noises of the world, and this he could do well. He was listening always for the voice of the spirit, for the one message that was of value. And the result was that sometimes his conversation was of an amazing depth. Even the learned among the priests said that his words seemed directly inspired, coming not from him, but from on high.

Everything that had any reference to the Passion drew him always. That was why he was so devoted to the writings of Saint Gertrude and of Catherine Emmerich, both lovers of the Passion. He often quoted from the life of Marie-Marthe Chambon, the lay Visitation Sister who had an especial devotion to the five wounds. This great love which animated his life was best exemplified in his own devotion to the Way of the Cross, which he made each evening no matter how worn out he might be or how late the hour he could give to it.

Those who made the stations with him left accounts of this evening devotion which completed his day. During the years the method varied but little. Upon his knees, on the stones close to the altar, he would spend an hour, hands joined with no support, lost completely in God. Never did he make the stations in a hurried or distracted way. At every station he bowed down a long time, and one would have said he was himself suffering the tortures of the Passion, so twisted were his features with pain. Sometimes he would talk of the Passion during his time in his office. The sight of the little Brother sunk in his chair, his eyes lowered, a crucifix in his hand, telling in detail of the sufferings of Our Lord was affecting for the pilgrims. In every fibre of his being he spoke that pain, and his tears and twisted features bore witness to how it affected him. It stirred the witnesses too, and it stirred many a heart and brought about conversions.

Brother André had an inner sense that told him when a hardened sinner was in his audience, and those were the times he selected for talks on the Passion. When he knew he was given the opportunity to conquer a sinner, Brother André paid no attention to time. Curious visitors who came as sightseers he could get rid of easily and did. But he never snubbed a sinner or hurried him along. When he knew he had a soul to bring back to Christ, time was no object with him. He would talk between his silences and with tears. "Oh, if you loved the good God," he would say pleadingly, "if you loved Him as He loves you! If you realised how sin crucifies Him over and over again!" More often than not, Brother André, named after one of Christ's first fishermen, would draw another soul into his spiritual net. "To pray well," he would often say, "you must think of Jesus on the Cross. That will make true prayer." And, with tears raining down his cheeks, he would insist, "Do you not see how impossible it is to be distracted when one sees his Brother crucified?"

Father Emile Deguire was one of his closest confidants for many years. He edited *The Annals* from 1923 through the next nine years. After that he was, until a year before Brother André's death, rector of the Oratory. For most of his stay at the Oratory he occupied the room next the one given Brother André and he was a witness to the lateness of the night work of the Brother, as his prayers still went on when most of the house was long since asleep.

Father Deguire would try to draw Brother André into talking of himself and his past, but that was a difficult thing to do, for the Brother was always timid and reserved, especially so with priests. But as he grew to know him better, he would often come into Father Deguire's room to tell him about some of his sick and the various ways in which Saint Joseph was caring for them. One day when the priest had read in a French publication some mention of the Notre Dame porter and of early cures said to be due to his intervention, Father Deguire mentioned the account to him. "Were there any before 1904, Brother?" he asked.

"Oh, yes," Brother André did not hesitate in replying, "many cures took place before that." He shook his head sadly. "But it was a great deal of trouble in those days. The doctors at the college during those years were greatly annoyed with me and put all sorts of hindrances in my way. The one who made the most trouble is long since dead. He died, poor man, and I could not help him."

Father Deguire smiled. "Well, then, perhaps it is not safe to oppose you?" Brother André remained serious. "It was the will of God," he said briefly. He came in one evening to Father Deguire's room. "I seem to be having a new kind of pilgrim these days," he said. "The stock market crash is evidently making people conscious, just as the war did, that there is something in the world besides the making of money—or the losing of it. They are so discouraged though, these people, more so it seems to me than a man with a paralysed leg or cancer."

"What do you tell them? Can you cure such a disease, Brother?" Brother André shrugged his shoulders. "I can only tell them that money is nothing, and that a man ought to worry about his soul instead. He might lose that too—and then what?" He got up and began to walk toward the door. He turned as he reached it. "Father," he said hesitatingly but with firmness too, "I hear you are going to put my picture in the next *Annals*. Please don't do it." But Father Deguire assured him it was only a group picture and he would be only one of six or seven people in it. So he submitted, but not very cheerfully. His real idea of art in the *Annals* was picture after picture of Saint Joseph.

One day he came in shaking his head. "Father Rector, the dresses some of these women wear—it is dreadful. There was a woman in my office today and I thought she had on a bathing suit instead of a dress. I told her so too"; and he smiled a bit maliciously. "And then came another one even worse, and I asked her if she had forgotten to put on her dress in her hurry to get here. It seemed to me I told her that if she expected to obtain any favour she would have to go and put a dress on first."

Before Father Rector could even agree with his annoyance, Brother André was off on another vexing matter connected with his women visitors. "They talk so much, some of them so very much. If they just wouldn't insist on telling their troubles with every little detail when there are so many waiting their turn! And then I get angry at them—and that doesn't help either. But, of course, they aren't all like that," he added, remembering his many good friends among the gentler sex. "But they do, many of them, talk too much." He rose suddenly. "I must go, Father. I have a great deal of praying still to do." "Why not go to sleep and offer to God this time. I am sure He would accept it from you as part of a continuous prayer, Brother." Brother André looked at him reproachfully. "Oh, I have to remember so many individuals in special prayers. When there are so many conversions as we have now and so many special favours obtained I want to mention each person by name. And that cannot be done in sleep."

Some of the visitors of later days were more than merely curious, even though they were in the class of sceptics. George Ham, who wrote a book about Brother André, himself saw two miracles and chronicled them soberly and with no attempt at any natural explanation. One was wrought for a woman from Plattsburg who had been on crutches for seventeen years. He saw her walk unaided to her car after she left Brother André's office. The other was in favour of a Miss Brooks who told Mr. Ham it was the first time in years that she had been able to use her limbs freely.

More and more doctors were certifying the cures too ; among them Dr. Campeau of Montreal, whose patient, Louis Bertrand, had been cured of an advanced cancer of the arm. Once a certificate came from a Protestant physician, who wrote in obvious astonishment of his patient, "She can walk normally with both legs, and it had been impossible without crutches."

Every year the pilgrims who came to the Oratory returned for another visit and worried for fear Brother André would be in heaven before they saw him again. But each year he was there to greet the newcomers as well as those who had come to him before ; the ones who had been cured in body and those whose cure was of the spirit only ; and the curiosity seekers, many of whom remained to pray though they had come only to stare.

Brother André's memory continued excellent and his eyesight remained keen. His memory for names, addresses and even for telephone numbers was little short of phenomenal, and he usually looked over his glasses rather than through them. At seventy-five, and even later, he was still washing up his own room and would let no one help him. He was still helping in the refectory when he was at home. And his mending he refused to let anyone do for him. In looks he had not changed much with the years. He was a little thinner, a little smaller, and a bit more bent. But his face was as full of life and love as ever. The French artist Vermare came to the shrine one day and Mr. Claude ushered him into the little office. Brother André looked up with a welcoming smile. The artist gave a gasp of astonishment.

"But you are my Curé of Ars. How remarkable a resemblance you have to that sainted man, Brother!" Brother André shook his head deprecatingly. "No, no, the resemblance is no doubt in our common French blood. But in his veins there flows also the blood of one of God's great saints." Mr. Claude told the visitor that perhaps there was another reason : "Brother André was born on the feast day of the Curé d'Ars, Monsieur."

Vermare had scarcely heard what they were saying. He was still lost in astonishment at the resemblance. "What a similarity in the faces—even in the expressions. Oh, Brother, I should like to mould your head as I did his." Brother André refused resolutely. He looked around hastily to make sure that no one in authority had heard this ill-advised remark ; for they were all very tiresome about photographs and paintings—and now a statue! That would be too much to bear.

As years passed Brother André still stood in his office every day just as he had from the beginning of his work. Only if he were away on a trip of some kind did Saint Joseph's clients fail to find him at his place ; his arms folded, a smile on his face. Year by year, too, he went daily to visit the old chapel and the great crypt over which the basilica of his dreams was rising. Every morning he was at his place behind the altar to receive Holy Communion. The laity seldom saw him there, for he remained hidden long after the early service was over. He always knelt there for a long time, his head on his arms, absolutely still, noticing nothing that went on about him.

His superiors entertained one great hope for him now : that the basilica would be completed before he died. Times were hard and money was coming in slowly. The work had been practically halted when the council of the shrine met on the first Wednesday of November, 1935, to discuss what should be done. The building was to go on only when there were funds to continue it : that had been the decision in the beginning and the decision must be kept.

The new rector of the Oratory, Father Cousineau, had accepted that office with the conviction that it would be out of the question to undertake the completion of the basilica for some years. He did not want, however, to hold up the work entirely, if at all possible. As they all sat down for the meeting, he felt sad that construction had to be interrupted at all and he was hoping that some way might be evolved to insure its continuance. But no one had any solution to offer, and an air of sadness came over the group around the table.

Brother André, sitting quietly among them, was the only one who did not look sad at all. He had, of course, no idea what the work was going to cost nor what a vast amount of money must still be collected to carry out the original plan, since for Brother André a few hundred dollars was still a sum large enough to start anything. He had no practical plan to offer them this time that was centred in dollars and cents. But he did say this : "You want to cover the basilica, don't you, and as soon as possible? Then why not place a statue of Saint Joseph within those open walls and he will find a roof for himself." They looked at one another. No one had thought of that, so taken up had they been with the problem of finding just the money to carry on.

That very afternoon of November, they went in procession to the basilica, climbing the steep hill to the church. Brother André started with them bravely, but part way up he had to stop. For some time now he had had recurrent attacks of what the doctors feared was an angina condition, and his heart would not permit any undue exertion like climbing. Smiling a bit sadly, he waved them on to finish the journey without him, while he sat down on a boulder and followed them with his eyes. Later two of the religious came back and found him rested, and with their help he reached the summit and breathlessly paused at the portico. In the hearts of those who had left him sitting part way up to the new building, there had been a presentiment of sorrow : the building would in time be finished, of course, none of them had any doubt of that—but would Brother André be there to see it? So they all welcomed him with smiles as he came to join them in the great dusty, empty building, the walls of which reached high in the air.

Father Rector put a statue of Saint Joseph inside the open walls, and prayers were recited. For Brother André and some of the others this was the third time that Saint Joseph had been carried in procession on Mount Royal. Over thirty years before Brother André had carried a statue all by himself up the hill and put it in the rocky protection his own hands had built. A few years later he had been one in a procession that carried a statue to the tiny chapel, just completed. And now, once more, Saint Joseph was borne to another building. This time it was for a definite purpose : he was to provide a roof for his building. At present he had no roof but the sky to protect him, as he stood on the spot in the basilica selected for him. But Saint Joseph was a strong saint, capable of enduring all weathers and also very capable at building shelters.

Brother André went to his room tired but happy. In the night he called out as if in pain, and the Brother who slept in the room next to his, fearing the old man might have had a heart attack, hurried in. He found Brother André unable to speak at first and his hands were clutching his throat.

"I think I dreamed it but I am not sure," he managed to gasp after a while ; "for it aches here so badly that I think it must have been real. It was the devil—he had me by the throat and was choking me."

When he felt better he smiled his mischievous smile. "So

he doesn't want a roof on the basilica, eh? And do you know what I managed to say to him when I got my breath back after his first attack? I said : 'Don't you think one could desire death so that one might go to see the good Lord?' And that ended it. He seized me just once more and then he fled."

Evidently Brother André had known exactly what was needed to stimulate building. Not more than two months after the gesture of faith had been made, obstacles which had seemed insurmountable were cleared away. Plans were gone over, permissions were granted, from the religious councils, from the archbishop, from the Apostolic Delegate, from Rome itself. A loan was raised. A new architect was selected to replace the one who had recently died.

Before Father Cousineau went to discuss the matter with the archbishop, he knocked at Brother André's door. "Pray hard," he bade him. "I am going to meet Archbishop Gauthier and ask his permission to continue construction."

"Have you a medal of Saint Joseph with you?" asked Brother André.

Father Cousineau shook his head, and Brother André began feeling in his pockets for one. There was always at least one there.

"While you are talking to the archbishop, Father, be sure to hold this firmly in your hand and don't worry. To hold a medal in one's hand makes one think more of Saint Joseph, than just wearing one. It is a sign of greater confidence. And don't worry at all. You will get the permission."

And Father Cousineau came back with the authorisation from His Excellency to continue the work immediately.

CHAPTER TEN

BUILDING THE BASILICA

WHAT was to prove Brother André's last visit to his beloved United States was a very happy one. Since there was need now of additional funds for the basilica's completion and especially for its dome, he felt he must bestir himself and help. He kept persistently asking for permission to make the trip, and finally received it, though his superiors hesitated for a long time, feeling he was too old and ill now for such extended journeys. For several years they had been uneasy about these lengthy trips, and a look at the frail old man was not calculated to make them less so. No doubt they were won over by his final argument. "But one shouldn't keep from travelling to do good," was the plea that won the permission.

On this trip he hoped to interest the Rockefellers in giving substantial help for getting the roof on the pavilion. Unfortunately they were both out of town, but Mr. John Burke gave him a goodly sum to offset his disappointment. At the home of the Ryans in New York City, where he was a guest, he spoke continually of this one desire of his—to see a roof on the basilica before he died. "It is the last worldly task I want to do," he told his hosts and their guests to whom he was presented. "But I am over ninety years old now and that is quite an age for planning worldly tasks." Mary Ryan assured him that the work would go on even if he were not there to see to it in person, for he would still be looking after it. "What I think, Brother," she said, "is that you will drop the roof down from Heaven through the prayers of the people whose dimes and quarters will put the roof on the basilica." He looked at her with his keen, penetrating eyes and thought that over a few minutes.

"Do you really think so?" he asked, and then he looked very happy.

The Ryans never had a guest they loved so to have with them. During the days he spent there they were always conscious of the mystic this fragile old man was; yet he was so delightfully eager about everything, and his mind worked so fast he saw a joke before it was fully spoken.

The second morning of his visit his hosts took him to the Church of the Blessed Sacrament to Mass, and afterward Mr. Ryan showed Brother André to the sacristy to meet Monsignor Keegan. Hardly were the introductions finished when Brother André was on his knees. "Your blessing, Monsignor," he said. But Monsignor Keegan lifted him to his feet and said smilingly, "Oh, far rather I should ask yours, Brother." Later when two young priests asked Brother André for his blessing he shook his head. "I am not a priest, you see, and so I cannot really give you my blessing." But, lest they be disappointed, he added, "I will give you my prayers." Mary Ryan had been at first greatly alarmed when her friend Mrs. Laporte telephoned from Montreal that Brother André was coming to New York and that she wished to confide him to the Ryan family care during his days there. "What does he eat?" she asked in a panic, remembering some of the stories she had heard of the old man's habits. A laugh came through the receiver. "Just keep some hard crusts of bread in a little pan on the back of the stove where they will keep dry, and have plenty of black coffee in a pot there too."

Miss Ryan was not entirely reassured. One might entertain angels unawares with a degree of ease, but to entertain a saint and do it knowingly was a very different matter. But she found she had been unduly alarmed, for during the three days of his visit he proved a model guest, considerate and thoughtful. She had heard that one of his nieces at whose home he sometimes stayed had said she liked to put out her very best bed comforts for him, but it made little difference to her uncle. In the morning his bed was utterly unmussed : he had chosen the floor instead.

On his first evening with them Miss Ryan, with some qualms, gave a dinner party for him. Four priests had been invited to meet him and he sat beaming at them each in turn, happy as a child and honoured to have them come to see him, never realising that they felt theirs was the honour in meeting him. She watched with some apprehension when Brother André was served, but she saw that he began to eat whatever was set before him, with no comment or protest. He ate and evidently enjoyed the slice of thick steak on his plate. Later, when the dessert was served, he looked at Miss Ryan, wondering if he should attempt it; then, meeting her eye, he smiled and set himself to eat it. The talk at table was easy and natural and Brother André joined in frequently, in his fluted voice broken now and then by laughter. When the subject of Communism came up, Brother André was especially vocal, for here was a subject that gave him great concern during his later days. "With the help of God and the help of Mary we shall surely conquer it finally," he said with deep earnestness. "Brother," asked one of the guests, "what do you think of the ills of our time. Will they cease soon?" His eyes grew sad. "Yes—they will end." "But when, Brother? The issues have been with us so long now—it seems endless." "Ah, when God is angry as He is now, then it takes time. The trouble is that the world isn't praying enough. So the remedy is really simple and within the world's grasp, too. More of us must pray. Instead of using this present economic crisis as a lesson, we keep forgetting God —and we blaspheme instead of praying. It will all end when we pray more."

After dinner Brother André learned that one of the guests, Father Theophane Maguire, was still suffering from an injured spine suffered years before as a missionary in China, and he offered to rub him. As he worked, Father Maguire said, "Pray for my soul, Brother, too." Brother André looked up and his eyes twinkled. "Better leave your spine injury with you, if I must pray for your soul," he retorted.

Next day Miss Ryan learned that her guest slept in the bed prepared for him. Later they went to a hospital to see a little boy with a very serious mastoid condition. Brother André took the bandaged little head in his wrinkled hands, held it straight and then rubbed it gently. The child who had been weeping with pain fell silent. Then, evidently feeling the pain ebbing at the gentle touch, he looked slyly from under his tear-brimmed lashes and smiled at the little old man who smiled back a gentle smile of gaiety and reassurance.

At the bedside of a woman suffering from phlebitis he stood very still for a few moments. "Do you feel well now?" he asked. "Is there any pain in your leg?" She looked alarmed at his question. "Yes, I have a little," she said.

Back in the car, Brother André said, "I wasted my time at that visit I am afraid. There must be faith on the patient's side as well as on mine, you see." And he went on to tell of a woman to whom he had been talking about the beauties of Paradise who said to him, "Just the same, Brother, we always have a fear of death." . . . "I told her that when one has lived a good life one needn't fear death, for it is the gate of Heaven, and she said, 'Perhaps so, but the sky is so far away.' And I told her there is such a little distance between the sky and the earth that God hears us always. I recited the Our Father in a very low voice, so I could hardly be heard, and I said, 'You see, the good God hears me—and that is a sign we are very close to Heaven'."

As they drove up Fifth Avenue the traffic delayed them often. Brother André sat quietly observing everything, then finally shook his head in mock irritation, and his eyes danced with merriment. "New York is too slow for me," he declared. Next morning he was taken to Mass in the church of Saint Francis of Assisi. After Mass he looked all around the church with great satisfaction. "There is great love and devotion here. I feel it all through me." When he was put on the train which was to take him to Providence next morning, the Ryans said good-bye to their guest with deep regret. They had been afraid they would have to entertain a Curé d'Ars who would insist on crusts and water and continuous prayers. Instead they found they had a model guest, who acceded to everything they wished, asking in return only to be taken daily to a church for at least an hour.

Brother André returned to the Oratory after having had a very pleasant time and looking younger than when he had gone away. He had brought money too, goodly offerings from friends to whom he had spoken of Saint Joseph's needs. Without counting it, he put it into the hands of his superiors. That part of the work would be handled by them. A dearer duty remained his own. When the crypt was quiet in the late evening of his return, he stole in and placed there the crutches and other physical aids he had brought with him, given by those who, after his visit, no longer had need of them.

On Christmas Eve he went to see the Laportes, partly to pay a visit to good friends of his, and partly to wish them a holy, happy Christmas. And he had a third reason : he wanted to tell them of the wonderful time he had had in the United States. "So many friends I have there and they helped me so much with the roof of the basilica." And he told them of the sums given him and the great interest the Catholics in the United States took in this far-away shrine that Brother André brought so close to them. One of the things that had particularly impressed him he had to share with the Laportes. "The Ryan family put a little shrine of Saint Joseph in my room. I knew when I came in that it was especially for me. And on the table there was a beautiful shrine of Lourdes, too. To wake and see Saint Joseph in that lovely place and so close to me—it was the nicest thing I saw on my whole trip."

The Laportes looked him over carefully. They decided he seemed none the worse for his trip. In fact they agreed with his fellow religious, that he looked better than ever, and younger. When he went away he was worrying about the roof over Saint Joseph. Now it was clear the roof was going to be begun soon. And Brother André knew very well that what Saint Joseph starts he always finishes. They looked at him, as he sat there talking animatedly, with love and with satisfaction. He was, for so old a man, such a very neat one. The cassock which he now wore constantly, in the house and on the street, was always spotlessly clean. It might be an old one, but it was immaculate always. He got up to leave for he had promised to rest before the midnight Mass. "I came to tell you especially what a wonderful time I had with your friends," he said. "And one of them in the United States asked me at a dinner, 'Brother André, how have you managed to be so old?' I told him how easy that was. I did it by eating as little as possible and praying as hard as possible."

He showed them before he left another gift he had brought with him. Miss Ryan had felt that Brother André, no matter how well Saint Joseph protected him or how able he was to care for himself, was too old to travel alone. So, for additional protection she offered him a first-class relic of the Little Flower. "Keep her watchful eyes over your travels," she said. "I have my medal of Saint Joseph," he assured her, but his glance showed he was eager for this relic, too. Then he looked at her sharply. "Are you sure it is a first-class relic?" She showed him the documents and when he had looked at them carefully he allowed her to fasten the relic to his watch chain and there it was when the train pulled out of the station. And there it still was when he showed it to the Laportes. When he had told his inquirer the reason for his successful old age—that it was mainly due to prayer—he spoke the truth. And the years had given him a spiritual insight built out of the hours on his knees. Those who thought that Brother André had little religious knowledge were shown their mistake quickly. Only a brief conversation was needed to indicate how he could enter on deep spiritual subjects with ease, and how often his simple comparisons were used only to establish and make the listener understand a deeper abstract truth. He never pretended to be a theologian. His praying remained always simple, and he loved best the vocal prayers used by everyone—the Rosary, the Aves, the novenas.

Secular conversations, even when very interesting, were for him only transitions that led him to the one subject which interested him—God. "He slips us a greeting," said one friend, "and then begins to speak of the supernatural." Politics he never mentioned or the public figures that filled the political scene, and when others spoke of such matters in his presence he appeared bored. His conversations dwelt mostly on the good Lord, and in every way he tried to lift people to Him. It was in the course of such discourses, always impromptu, that his visitors saw the soul of a saint in all its height and depth. When, with eyes lowered or half shut, he spoke for some twenty minutes at a time of the Passion of Christ, more than one listener felt a revived love for his Faith and it carried more than one of them from Brother André's little office straight to the confessional in the crypt.

He knew how to make the Faith practical too. "Do you

love the good Lord?" Brother André would interrogate one of his visitors. "Yes," came the answer, but perhaps with some hesitation. "What proofs of love do you offer Him? How many times, for example, do you go to Communion? Every week perhaps?" "Oh, from time to time. I don't know just how often."

Brother André looked amazed. "But when you have an intimate friend, do you spend weeks and months without going to see him, without giving him signs of your affection when he lives very near to you? And when Jesus loves you so—when He gave you the deepest proof of it by dying for you. . . ." Tears rolled down the wrinkled cheeks and many listeners were so moved they wept with him.

There were those who came only to ask a temporary favour but were so impressed by the way in which Brother André spoke of divine love that it changed their whole concept of religion, and they went away forgetting what they meant to ask of him. "I understand my duties as a Christian as never before," said one man as he left the Oratory, "and I am going to Communion every day and make an effort to teach all those about me to love God." He wrote the same thing later to Brother André. That was the sort of thanksgiving letter he liked best of all to receive.

It was not that he thought the approach to religion must be always sombre. None could better dispense jokes and smiles than he when he chose, and he knew that it was sometimes wise and right to be very gay about the Faith. But he knew too with Saint Joseph, that often the deepest seriousness is the right way to heal souls and find the way to hearts.

Not miracles but the progress of souls he preferred to speak about and to hear about. And knowing the way to that was by prayer, he joined his prayers always with those who came to him. He prayed with ardour for all who came to solicit favours.

One evening he led a blind young man into the almost empty

crypt. He left him in one of the pews, and then went forward and knelt on the pavement of the church and began to pray. He mounted the steps of the choir and prayed again. Finally he went up the steps which led to the foot of the altar and, kneeling on each one, continued his petitions. It was as if he were storming Heaven for help for the man who knelt behind him.

Once a woman with both legs inert was carried into his office and Mr. Claude, seeing how bad her condition was, made others yield place to her and the men who were carrying her. Brother André saw her. Instead of the usual formula, he stood with his eyes closed, deep in prayer. Then across the narrow office his voice suddenly rose. "Get up and walk."

"No, no, Brother," she protested. "I can't. Both my legs are completely paralysed. Brother, truly I can't do it."

He shook his head. "Must I do the praying for you and you do none of it? Must I alone have faith? But you must have some or you would not be here. Woman of little faith, I order you—to get up and walk." While the crowd waited breathless, she suddenly freed herself from the men who were supporting her and stood erect. Tears of joy filled her eyes. Her step, as she came closer to Brother André, was firm and sure. He smiled at her—a tired smile. "I had to pray hard to give us enough faith," he said.

But there was no doubt about the miracles—not cures like this of the lame or the blind, but the deeper miracles of the soul reborn. Of course many cures never received the publicity given to some. Their very nature precluded it. But had Brother André done no more than draw the sick to him on the mountain top and give them faith to live, even if crippled or unseeing the material world, he would have done a mighty work, for he taught thousands of his visitors, the sick in body and the sick of soul, how they needed God, and what God could do for them. Though with those whose sincerity he recognised he was always patient and kind, it was very different when someone came in to see him whose intention was not good. He could tell these, too, often to their discomfiture.

Once a boarding house keeper came to complain that her house was losing patrons and no more were coming in. Friends had suggested she go to see Brother André. Finally she did, though she had herself never thought highly of him—a fact she had never uttered aloud and so thought no one knew it. Brother André listened to her long story; listened to the end. "When you stop thinking badly of me and the Oratory," he told her when she had finished, "your boarders will come back." The woman, at first utterly surprised, became angry. But, after a little silence, she looked at him and said, "I am ashamed to say that it is really true." She went quietly away.

When a young girl came to Father Dion he sent her, as he often did in such cases, to Brother André. There were five in the family, she told the Brother, and their parents were dead. The eldest brother was guardian for the rest, and now he wanted to get married. She had come to ask the prayers of the Oratory that he would not marry. But when she saw Brother André she did not tell the whole story, only that she came to ask his prayers.

"But for what?" he wanted to know.

"Just for my intentions." She could not hide her deceit.

"But your intentions are not good. Your brother doesn't need to lose his whole future for your sake. It is perfectly all right for him to get married if he wishes to. Better pray for something for yourself—say for a good conscience. I will pray with you for that."

Once Mr. Claude found a blind man weeping aloud in the little chapel. He looked up at Mr. Claude's sympathetic question. "I have come from far away to seek a cure."

"Have you been to see Brother André?"

"Yes, and he told me to come and pray in the church. I have followed his counsel but without success."

"Then go back and see him again," suggested Mr. Claude. Later he asked Brother André if the blind man had gone away without a cure. "Do you know him?" asked the Brother.

"No, he is an utter stranger to me. I merely spoke to him to comfort him because he was weeping so hard."

Brother André shrugged. "Well, there is no likelihood of his being cured. He didn't tell you he is living with another man's wife, did he? Let him look to that first."

He liked to engage in teasing, especially what he called supernatural teasing. Once when he came into his office he was greeted by one of the nuns of the Congregation who asked him what book he was carrying. He opened it for her inspection and she peered at the small letters. "I can see it is a *Following of Christ* by the words at the top, but the tiny letters of the script —how can you ever decipher them? I certainly can't."

"Oh, it's easy. Try this page."

"I'm sorry, Brother. I've broken my glasses and can hardly see anything without them."

"Try it anyway," he insisted. To please him she did, and was amazed to find she could read the print very easily. But later, when she tried it with a book in her own room, the power was gone.

After she had gone Brother André sat down for a few precious minutes before more people came in and, with his glasses as usual on the top of his head, he pored over the fine print in the book, spelling carefully along the paragraphs. He had studied some of this book so much that he knew a great deal of it by heart. Sometimes he showed cherished portions to a vistor—especially those which dealt with the inner life. "They can maintain the thought of God in the midst of absorbing worldly occupations when they read that," he often said. He enjoyed mere natural teasing occasionally. His mind remained in his very last year clear and able, and his wit was, as it had always been, pointed. He answered the telephone in his office one day when no one else was with him. "When is the eight o'clock Mass?" he heard a woman's voice ask. "For you, madame," he said promptly, "it is at nine o'clock."

When an officer one evening stopped the car in which Brother André was riding, because it was going far too fast— he had in fact been urging the driver to go faster—the old man leaned forward. "What's your name, officer?"

"Lamouche, Brother."

"Well, it's much too late in the year for flies,"—*mouche* means fly—said Brother André and settled back happily in his seat.

"What is that man's name?" he asked Mr. Claude one day after a man had gone away cured.

"Laverdure, Brother." *Verdure* stands for fresh, new grass.

"Good—*il a reverdi*," "he has grown fresh and green again," he chuckled.

Sometimes his silence counted for as much as his words. One evening when he and Mr. Laporte came home from visiting the sick in the city at a late hour, Brother André said he must get back as soon as possible, for he had some special prayers to say. So the car was speeded up and no one looked at the speedometer as they raced along. Suddenly a motor cycle was heard puffing up. When it came abreast the car off jumped a policeman.

"Where are you going at this rate?" he asked with chill politeness.

Mr. Laporte answered as non-committally as possible. Brother André meantime had been sunk in the corner of the car but now came forward a little. The officer caught sight of the little

Brother, sitting so quietly, his eyes twinkling, and recognised him. His eyes opened in a surprised stare and he flushed as if he were the guilty person. Then he turned, got on his motor cycle again, and rode off without a word. And Brother André got his prayers said in time.

In some matters the Congregation occasionally had trouble with this miracle worker. Not in ordinary matters of obedience, but rather from the fact that he took the duties of a lay Brother too seriously for himself. He would, for instance, insist on waiting on the priests at table when he was at home. This bothered them, especially the younger men. Father Murphy used to complain to him about it, feeling Brother André was too old and too important and too busy with other things to wait on him. They had a little private feud about it, but the result was always the same : in the end Brother André would be serving him at table very serenely, and Father Murphy would, fuming inwardly, allow himself to be served.

One day he came up to him and spoke persuasively. "Look, Brother André, you look very tired. Won't you rest a bit more?" For once Brother André did not argue the matter. "I am tired," he said. "I don't think I will last long."

Father Murphy had not expected that this would be the result of his solicitude.

"Oh, of course you will, Brother. You will see the dome on the basilica. You must wait for that." He shook his head. "No, I won't see it. I won't see it finished. I longed to. But I'm too old and I'm really not needed now."

Father Labonté came up as they were talking. This priest was one of those very close to Brother André who understood him well. He once summed up the lay Brother's life in a single phrase that was almost a biography. "He is always before God," he said of him.

As he came up he caught the last words to Father Murphy.

They were discouraging words and not like him, so he resolved to give Brother André something else to think about. "Brother, I want to speak to you about my sister. She has been bedridden now for about eight years and is in an advanced state of tuberculosis. Only recently have I learned how bad her condition is. Do you think you could help her?" Brother André listened carefully and asked a few questions; then he nodded his head and the old light was in his eyes. "I will do the impossible for her," he assured Father Labonté.

He still kept a careful check on domestic matters about the crypt and the chapel. When he came home from a sick visit he always made sure that the windows and doors were locked and all the lights out. It made him increasingly displeased to have someone forget to turn out lights. Anything wasted was so much taken from Saint Joseph's money. The year before his death, coming home from a visit, he found a single light still burning in the church. He put it out and sought the porter.

"Are you expecting a visitor?" he asked that sleepy official.

"Of course not, Brother André. What makes you ask?"

"Because the crypt is still illuminated."

He loved his Oratory and loved to see it in excellent condition, but extravagance there or elsewhere he never condoned.

"Don't eat that old bread, Brother," a confrère said to him when he was almost ninety and feeling very ill.

"If I don't it will be wasted," he said and went on eating.

But he never wanted any money saved when it came to increasing the building. Then he wanted to give with both hands, and he loved only to have them empty so that he could ask to have them filled again. When he came home from a trip, no matter how fast he had wanted to drive, he asked to go slowly when he saw the Oratory. Once there had been only a little wooden chapel and a wooden walk. Now there was a great sweep of flower beds bordered by tall French poplars

instead of that crooked walk. As one came to the street entrance
•there were two granite kiosks with a portico joining them. Just
inside was the great monument to Saint Joseph, offering a
welcome at the door of his home to the incoming pilgrims,
speeding the home-going ones with his blessing. About him
stood four stone angels, representing Church, Knowledge,
Country, Labour.

A great lawn sloped upward to the crypt, and the unfinished
basilica that looked as if it were a hill of granite in the mountain
itself. Against dark trees, blue sky and grey mountain, it made
a beautiful picture, even for eyes less loving and devoted than
those of Brother André. And, when he reached the end of the
steps and looked past the monastery, there was still his own
shabby chapel on which to bestow the last look of all. Though
he had his own room in the monastery now, and had had for
years, he loved to go to pray in his little chapel with the stained
ex-votos and its memories of happy years in co-operation with
Saint Joseph.

CHAPTER ELEVEN

BROTHER ANDRÉ GOES HOME

To all who knew him it was evident that Brother André was failing fast. The heart attacks were more frequent and he was feebler than he had ever been and for longer intervals. After all, he was over ninety years old.

In October of 1936, while M. Chartier was working on a bust of him, they spoke together, as they usually did, of the work on the basilica. This was the best way to keep Brother André satisfied while he posed. But this time he looked sad when the sculptor spoke of it. "Oh, the continuation of the work is assured," he said. "But I—it is different with me. I am not needed now. It is time for me to go."

A little later in the year Father Clement said to him, "You see the people were right when they said you would live to see your basilica." Brother André shook his head. "Ah, Father Clement, you have never once heard me say I would see it finished."

The priest's face was sad when he left the old man—and that was something that happened very rarely, for Father Clement was gaiety itself. The sick liked to go to his office for it was always a cheerful place when he was in, and a pleasant place to wait. Joy and charity, everyone agreed, were mixed in him in exactly the right proportion. But that one day he sat in his office with no smile on his face.

At the midnight Mass of Christmas of that year Brother André was kneeling behind the altar, his face in his hands, praying without moving as was his wont. He was able to assist at the second Mass, but before the end of the third he had to go to his room to rest. But everyone noticed that his face was bright and joyous as he went out supported by Brother Osèe. The tired, drawn look it had worn lately was entirely gone and he looked almost young again.

"What were you thinking of that made your face so happy, Brother?" Father Clement wanted to know later. He smiled at his old friend. "Oh, that in a year or two the Feast of Christmas will be celebrated in the basilica."

"And you will live to be a part of it, Brother."

"Oh, that—that doesn't matter. I have done all I had to do. The work doesn't need me any more."

"Oh, come, Brother, the Oratory still needs you."

"Perhaps, perhaps. But if one can do good on earth, just think how much more he can do in heaven."

A few weeks before he had expressed to Father Clement a fear of his, and this time a wholly imaginary one. He thought his superiors were planning to send him away from the Oratory to some other city.

"I can't do much more of course," he said, "but if it comes about I can always find some work to do no matter where I am."

Father Clement was sure he was mistaken and, after inquiries, was able to assure him that he was. Brother André looked relieved, but all he said was, "Well, I didn't really care what work they had for me or where they would send me to, Father, just so it helped the Community."

During that week he had a very severe attack, which was diagnosed as acute gastritis. New Year's Eve he was rushed to the hospital at Saint-Laurent. He was not nearly so worried as the rest of the staff at the Oratory was, for when he was lying on the stretcher waiting to be carried to the ambulance, he smiled at the people who were wrapping him up carefully against the cold. "I must look like a man leaving for the North Pole," he said. But when he reached the hospital, he had stopped smiling and jesting. When they had him safely in bed, he said to the nursing Sister who bent over him : "The Great Almighty is coming."

He obeyed the orders of the doctors willingly, as he always did, but was careful to tell them that he put his trust in God. "I have gone to see doctors during my life more through obedience than confidence in remedies," he said. Then he smiled his own twinkling smile. "But I do listen to them."

The next day a visiting priest stopped by his bed and said urgently, "Brother André, why don't you ask Saint Joseph to heal you?" He shook his head. "I can do nothing for myself," he said simply. "And then, see how much he has done for me," he added, his face lighting up. "People don't realise all that the good God is doing through the Oratory. I am not a lawyer, doctor, or a priest, but God has helped me with my work despite that. See His power."

That evening he called for his nurse. He was very patient in his pain and tried not to cause any trouble, and when he had to call a nurse repeatedly to his bed, he used to say to her, "It is your old nuisance ringing again. Sister, please do this for me. Rub me with this medal of mine. That will be more profitable for this pain than all those pills and injections. Rub hard."

After she had rubbed him for a while with the old worn medal he had often used for his sick, he stopped her. "It is strange. I feel no change at all. When I rub the sick, there is always something that gets better."

"That is because those people need a miracle to increase their faith—but not you," the nurse told him. He smiled at her. "That is true, Sister."

When Father Clement came in to see him, he was shaking his head at his arm, which had suffered a slight stroke that morning and was paining him a great deal. "My arm is a Communist," he told him. "The wicked thing hates me!"

Father Clement nodded. He knew all Brother André's feelings about Communism. He knew that was why Brother André wanted more and more devotion paid to Saint Joseph the workman ; and he was sure it was because of Saint Joseph the workman, and Saint Joseph of Mount Royal that Canada had been protected from the revolutions of other countries.

Brother André was following his thought. "Such people have no faith or law—people who live just for a realisation of their personal interests. Sometimes I actually pray that God will send them an illness so during it they will ponder, and before they die will be converted." He told Father Clement about the medal. "Several years ago my old sick sister told me to heal her, for I knew how much she was suffering. She said that I healed all the world and could do nothing for her. And that was true—I could not help her. So I told her that it was not I who cured but Saint Joseph ; and I said to her, 'Suffer instead, endure for the love of God'." So now he, who had all his long life preached the doctrine of accepting suffering and even being grateful for it, set himself to practising with a holy patience what he had preached to others.

When his superior was leaving, the Brother asked him, "Tell me, how is the Holy Father? I have been wondering if he is suffering much." When assured the Holy Father was better, he smiled. "Everyone must pray a great deal for him," he said urgently. While he lay there he composed a prayer which he said he wanted many of the people he knew to have, and one of the Sisters copied it for him. "Oh, good Saint Joseph, do for me what you would do if you were yourself in my place on the earth with a large family and a difficult business to administer. Good Saint Joseph of Mount Royal, help me and listen to me."

"A universal prayer," said his superior when he heard it. "The Holy Father and the humblest workman alike could say it."

"Do you know what I am doing, Father?" Brother André said. "I am offering my sufferings and my prayers for poor Spain. That terrible war—brother against brother. And only our prayers can put a stop to it. Tell me, Father," he changed the subject to ask eagerly, "is the building going on all right?"

The superior assured him it was progressing in spite of cold weather. They had thought they must stop for a little while, but had gone ahead anyway.

"Yes, tell them not to worry. We shall succeed. The temple of Saint Joseph will be completed. Come closer for a moment, Father." The voice was growing weaker now, for there was no longer strength for much exertion. When the priest bent over him, he said softly, "I just wanted to say once more how good God is. How powerful! How beautiful! For He must be beautiful since the soul which is only a ray of Him is so beautiful. Oh, Father," there was a touch of the old energy, "if the people only loved the good Lord, they wouldn't sin. Everything would go well if they only loved the good Lord as He loves us."

Next day Father Clement coming in for his daily visit found Brother André sunk in thought, his face lighted by a beatific smile. "What makes you so happy, Brother?" he asked.

"I have just been thinking about Heaven and how lovely it is. Think, Father Clement, only a veil separates us from the good God. You know," he added hurriedly, "it is not necessary to wish for death to go and see the good God."

During the week he received visitors constantly, although the nurses limited them as much as they could. He kept up his gaiety and his clear mind. At the least service rendered him he showed he knew it was rendered. On the fourth of January the nurse heard him murmur, "Mary, my sweet Mother, be my advocate and help me." Then very faintly, "Saint Joseph"— the rest she could not understand because the whisper was too weak. By the next morning he was in a coma. Extreme Unction was administered, but he did not recover consciousness.

And now, since it was evident that the end was very near, the Sisters permitted the people who had been clamouring to see him to enter the room in the little hospital. Most of Montreal had discovered where Brother André had been taken and a great many of them were waiting patiently for hours outside in the hope of seeing him once more. All that day and the next, until his actual death, a flow of visitors passed by his bed, some of them with crutches, or with faces pale from illness. Each came up in silence and touched him with some pious object on the old hands which had rubbed and healed so many.

He seemed to be sleeping peacefully as crowds passed—old men and young, women and girls, even small children, their lips murmuring a prayer, their eyes intent on the quiet little figure that did not see them.

For over forty years he had received daily sick and suffering people. Now, when he himself lay ill to death, it was very fitting that he should still be receiving them. Some had a rosary or a medal, some held out a crutch, but everyone touched some object to the thin hands stretched out on the coverlet. Even the priests and Brothers who came to look at him took off their crucifixes and touched them to his body. He lay with his eyes closed, not aware of them, lying as if asleep. The pain was gone entirely and his face was peaceful. The only unreal thing about him was that the twinkling eyes were now closed, never to open again.

It was the Eve of the Epiphany, a joyous day, but many in Montreal did not rejoice. They were listening on the radio to hear the latest word about the little Brother. Whole families were on their knees. It was as if a member of the family, or a dear friend, were dying—for he had been the friend and benefactor of all. In the churches men and women and children knelt in prayer and the burden of their prayer was—"Saint Joseph, save Brother André. He healed me." Or perhaps he had healed someone's brother or mother or child. Or perhaps it had been a spiritual healing that carried a sufferer over hard days into peace again.

His confrères refused to believe he was dying. They felt, as they always had, that he must see the basilica finished before he was called. But the doctors shook their heads and said he had only a few hours of life left. It was almost midnight when they recited the prayers for the dying and then the litany for the dying, and last the litany of Saint Joseph. The watchers about the bed, friends and confrères, listened to the sick man's breathing become more quiet, more easy, and their hopes rose. But suddenly it became very laboured, and fifteen minutes after midnight the doctors pronounced him dead.

They looked at the small, still face and began to intone the *Te Deum* as he lay there. He had died quietly, as gently as he had lived. He was done now with healing, for he was himself in the presence of the Great Healer. "I have asked God," he said to Father Clement shortly before being taken to the hospital, "to keep me always in front of Him, as the saints in Heaven." So his journey was not a far one.

On the Feast of the Epiphany, after the mortuary mask was moulded, and the heart had been removed from the body, Brother André was taken home to the Oratory again. As he entered the gates, the bells of the church and the college tolled for him. The nearer the body with its attendants approached Mount Royal, the greater became the crowd. When the crypt was reached it had become a solemn procession. The remains were placed in a side chapel and the great crowd sang the *Magnificat* before his body.

Father Cousineau gave a brief sermon on the work of Brother André and also gave the Congregation an account of the way in which his last hours had been spent. The body had been placed in a simple coffin of wood covered with a black cloth, and when Father Cousineau ceased speaking the people began to press forward for a last look at Brother André.

All that week they came, the crowds growing larger and larger each passing day. The weather was very bad, for it was a season of melting snow and ice-covered walks, and sometimes it rained—a cold sleety rain. But they kept coming, a continuous procession, taking a last look at the small figure, touching it with crucifix or beads. The church doors remained open all night. It was past midnight before the crowds had gone and it was not yet daylight when others came.

The funeral ceremonies took place the third day after his death at Montreal cathedral, after which he was taken home once more. And again men and women and children formed in procession and followed the coffin back to the church, through a bitter wind and over walks still icy.

This time, before the coffin was taken up the mountain, a pause was made at the college at its foot. The coffin was carried inside and placed in the very spot where in other days Brother André's little office had been. Around it gathered the old men who had been young men with him long ago, who knew him as no others did, and without whose help no doubt the burden he had borne would sometimes have been too heavy for his frail shoulders.

There was Brother Abondius who had helped him build, with his skilful hands, the first little shrine. There were several who had stood by him and comforted him in the days when he was suspect even among some of his own Congregation. There was Father Adolphe Clement, whose eyes, healed so many years ago, were now blind with tears as he looked down at his old friend. Then the boys of the school came by twos and stooped to touch the body. When they had gone Brother

André resumed his journey up the mountain—his last procession there, the last time he would lead his clients to Saint Joseph.

He lay in state in the crypt, in the niche where the crutches and ex-votos hung. It was a fitting place for him to lie, for the prayers of those he had healed were thick about him.

On Sunday the crowds were densest of all. Trains brought pilgrims from all over Canada and from the United States. Cars and buses and automobiles brought them so that at one time there were over a hundred thousand people present. The wide esplanade was black with them all day long, as they stood there waiting their turn, waiting for as long as five hours, to touch for a second the body of the dead man. It was a living flood of veneration and trust and faith.

The people were admitted two by two, and when they reached the body, filed in single lines. They went by at the rate of a hundred a minute. There seemed no end to them. There were cripples and blind there and every kind of sick, even to a man who was dying and who was brought in on a stretcher. There were conversions too : some known, many no doubt known only to God. One woman was weeping as she left the coffin. "I was not worthy to come so close to him," she said as she went away, and more than one asked if any of the confessionals were open. The great crowds were like a silent testimony that human beings follow sainted lives because in them they see the grandeur of heaven personified. Nearly a million people had come during that week to pay their last respects to the saintly little Brother.

Years earlier a visitor to Montreal come from France had asked the archbishop in some surprise, "Who is this Brother André that everyone seems to be talking about?"

"He is a man of God," said Archbishop Gauthier instantly. "And at his death I think we shall see half Montreal hastening to his tomb."

The people were now fulfilling that prophecy. Man of God he was to them, very evidently. In fact, the conviction one gathered from them was that Brother André was already a saint, and they treated his remains as they would those of one already canonized. A journalist who came to the mountain while Brother André still lay there said frankly, "I was of the number who thought they were too intelligent to be upset by Brother André. I would have regretted it all my life had I not been present during this week at his tomb."

Some who had, like the journalist, come through curiosity remained profoundly touched. The priests at the Oratory could have told more than one story of obstinate hearts long closed to God that opened to grace during that week.

On Tuesday, just before the final services, the body was taken from the church and left before the main door so that those who were unable to gain entrance previously could see him once more. Then, back in the crypt again, the office of the dead was begun. It was not so much, however, an office of the dead as the burial of a saint. And many of the clergy attending felt that the white vestments used for saints would have been more appropriate than the black ones of death.

Bishop Limoges officiated and Cardinal Villeneuve of Quebec gave the panegyric. "With all respect to Holy Church," said His Eminence, "we may say that today we celebrate the feast of humility. So little in his own eyes," he glanced down at the dead man before him, "without any suspicion of the throngs his death would brings together. We stress the doctrine of humility, for it is humility that we have paid homage to for the past week in this church, too small to hold us all. *Pauper*— that is to say poor : the religious we so often came to see at the Oratory. *Servus*, servant : the Brother, the last in rank in his community. *Humilis* : so little in his own eyes with no suspicion of the things his death would bring. You will agree with me that it was a triumph through the Cross. To him poverty was more than riches, to serve was sweeter than to be served.

"He was aged and weary," he said later in his sermon, "yet he could make others strong." And he ended, "No prince of the Church could have a funeral such as this, which affects the inmost sentiments of the heart, as we can testify today. Remember Brother André's words and hear him repeating them to us still : '*Ite ad Joseph*'."

After the absolution the remains were taken to the burial place—the small chapel where he had been placed the previous week, and put in a granite sarcophagus. The body had remained flexible during all the seven days, though out of respect it had not been embalmed. In the afternoon Archbishop Gauthier came to preside over the entombing ; and again a few of his closest friends through the years had one more glimpse of Brother André's face. Then the lid was closed down for the last time.

*   *   *

Barely a year had passed since the meeting of the Guardians of the Shrine when Brother André had told them, "If you wish a roof for the basilica, then place a statue of Saint Joseph within the walls and he will soon provide a shelter for himself." And Saint Joseph had done so, for the dome was over the basilica.

One autumn afternoon at the year's end a group of the Congregation walked together to the apse of the new building. They were celebrating the hoisting of the first stone for the roof. There were no special ceremonies or gathering of the faithful, but some two hundred workmen joined in the prayers before Saint Joseph's statue. The Rosary was recited, the litany of Saint Joseph followed, and the canonization of Brother André was earnestly prayed for. In January of 1941 the last stone was hoisted for the dome, and the laying of the arched ribs to cover it was begun.

One other of Brother André's dear hopes was being fulfilled. He had always hoped the Stations of the Cross would soon be erected, for he felt that many conversions would result therefrom, more even than the basilica would bring. Now, in the same year, the Stations were also built. Paths were laid out by a skilled landscape artist, so beautifully planned that the wooded hill was left intact and the small bushes and wild flowers remained. The paths ran among the birches and maples; stone steps were built here and there where the ground was especially hilly, and at the end of every narrow footpath stood a wooden cross, which was later to be replaced by a station carved from red granite.

In the little hall adjoining Brother André's room Mr. Claude still waited for pilgrims, but a few months after Brother André's death he changed his waiting place to the little hall that led to Brother André's own small room in the old chapel where he had first met him. Very kind and gentle, still loving Brother André's sick ones because he had so loved Brother André, he talked with them and tried to help them as much as he could. In the little office Brother André's heart had been placed in a glass container and it stood on his old desk where the pilgrims might see it as they passed by and touch it with their hands. And on the wall hung a picture of him, the old smile on his face as he watched the people come and go.

Not long after Brother André's death, Mr. Claude asked permission to come with a group of the Brother's intimate friends to commemorate the death of their friend on each first Wednesday of the month at his tomb. The first meeting brought not only the friends but more than a thousand people besides, and every month since then has seen the church filled at that hour.

On Friday evenings too, there were large crowds at the devotions, even though Brother André was no longer there in person. This was the devotion begun in the early days at the college, and performed mainly after supper because he had no time for extensive devotions before then, either because of his porter's work or because he had been in the village to see people who were sick. The few friends who had joined him sometimes then, had grown into the large group at the little chapel, and now they had increased to great crowds. Many came still who had come during his lifetime—those who knew that he had selected that day because of his love for the sufferings of Christ, which made it a very appropriate day for the stations.

During his last years he had more than once, when he felt especially tired and weak, worried because he thought he was too old to be of use, and that he was only in the way. But he never ceased to be hopeful too. "If they gave me another work somewhere else I'd be content. With a little rest I can still fulfil other tasks to help the community.

One look at the great shrine, at the great stone pile which prayer and love erected, will show whoever looks that Brother André did not have to be sent elsewhere because he was too old to be useful, or that he even needed a short rest in heaven before he began working again. He never ceased to work.

On August 9th, the ninety-second anniversary of Brother André's birth, the fresco over his tomb was blessed. Monsignor Dubuc performed the ceremony of dedication and Father Deguire, superior of the college, gave the sermon. The Masses began very early and all were crowded. Later in the day the Stations of the Cross were dedicated and at night there was a great torchlight procession.

In 1940 a greater celebration of the day was begun. A novena was held from the beginning of August to his birthday. Every evening a great torchlight procession took place and drew thousands of visitors from all over Canada and the United States. As many as ten thousand persons carried tapers and participated. For loveliness and grandeur the sight was unequalled. Led by the Cross, the pilgrims came marching eight abreast along the pavement in front of the crypt, and walked until they reached the street, then marched along Queen Mary's Road until they arrived at the right entrance of the shrine and began climbing the mountain. There were so many that often the leaders of the procession would find themselves back at the starting place before the rear of the procession had passed the church.

Other thousands preferred watching the glowing spectacle instead of being a part of it. To stand on the crypt roof and watch myriad points of light, moving, and listen to the hymns and prayers, was like seeing and reciting a great rosary of jewels with the Cross at its beginning.

After the procession had ended, the pilgrims grouped themselves in a glittering mass on the mountain. There, at the very top of the stairs, a beautiful altar had been erected for Benediction. A mighty *Tantum Ergo* rose from thousands of throats, and the words of the priest were clear in the night. When Our Lord was raised over them all in Benediction, a sigh went through the air as the great crowd bent in adoration.

Not only in the pleasant days of summer have the ceremonies at the shrine drawn great crowds. In 1941 on the Feast of Saint Joseph, a wonderful celebration was planned which was to go on continually for two days and a night. When the time came the weather was bitterly cold. The wind was icy and piercing, and the snow that fell became almost a blizzard sweeping down the slopes of Mount Royal. This did not deter the pilgrims any more than it did the Fathers and Brothers of Holy Cross.

There had been a novena held before the actual ceremonies.

On the 18th of March the doors of the crypt were never closed. The highways were crowded with cars and thousands came on foot. The many who could not find seats stood packed close to each other, and all their faces were turned in one direction— to the high altar where Saint Joseph stood with the Child in a mass of lilies. And everywhere there blossomed hundreds of flowers and hundreds of lighted candles.

At midnight, Mass over, twenty-five thousand Communions were received ; and surely in spirit Brother André was kneeling in his old place back of the altar and smiling at the wonderful evidences of devotion. Mass followed Mass after that, and hymns were chanted continually until dawn. Then the entire congregation, both those inside the church and those who were not able to find room to enter stood and sang the *Pater Noster* together.

There has been no end to the pilgrimages and no limit to their size. By motor bus, by train, in private cars, and on bicycles they come. Sometimes only a dozen together, sometimes four thousand in one pilgrimage. In summer Mass is often celebrated on the roof of the crypt which forms a cathedral whose vault is the sky.

Once in August, the sleeping occupants of the shrine were awakened at early dawn by the sound of prayers and hymns coming nearer and nearer. When the singers began to arrive it was not yet four o'clock, and by five there were fifteen thousand men waiting—and still singing. Huge as is the crypt, it could not hold them all and so the rest filled the narrow road leading to the slope and the great hall of the basilica. Mass was celebrated on the steps of the basilica in the warm sweetness of the August morning.

There was one pilgrimage of two hundred Catholic Iroquois Indians, and their Mass was celebrated by Father Michel, a Jesuit who was himself an Iroquois. The Mass was sung in that tongue, and those who listened thought they had never heard Gregorian chant take on such loveliness.

Sometimes the pilgrims were a group of farmers or Daughters of Saint Anne, or little boys and girls from some nearby parish, or perhaps an entire parish with its pastor. There has been no end to the variety of the groups which make up the pilgrimages, for they range from a following grouped around a single leader to the throngs that in the summer fill stair and roof with the confused sound of a multitude praying.

The favourite time for pilgrimages has of course always continued to be Brother André's birthday. The other great festivals owe their importance to history and time. But this is a day primarily of memories. Many of the pilgrims in other years had gone to see the lay Brother before they went into the church to pray. Many had been recipients of his own devotion to Saint Joseph. His little office was now a dear memory, a loving souvenir of him, and many of those who came to the shrine after his death thought, as they stood there, that they could still hear his fluted voice saying the familiar words, "Make a novena to Saint Joseph. Rub yourself with the medal." They crowded the little chapel on his day, and looked through tears at the white altar and the ex-votos of earlier days. His old friend Mrs. Laporte echoed the general feeling of them all : "I always feel a vacancy in my heart and life since his passing."

But neither in chapel nor office was the little black figure waiting for his clients. In the office his heart stood in its case on his desk. In the chapel his little housekeeping effects were still as he had left them and the few books he read and loved lay on the shabby table. In the office was the bust in bronze which was made of him during the last months of his life. On the wall back of the heart was his photograph with his signature in childishly rounded letters at the bottom The pilgrims who looked at it affectionately said it was very like him, for it wore the expression, kind yet warning, which he had on his face when he said, "Many of the sick do not obtain the health asked for because of their lack of faith and their fear of submitting to the will of God. For you know it is necessary to have faith when you rub yourself with the medal or with the oil."

Mr. Claude was still on hand to receive pilgrims, but Father Clement had gone to join Brother André. The death of his confrère of years weighed heavily on the priest and the Community sent him to Europe on a trip—his first. He saw the Holy Father and the ancient monuments of Rome and the lovely land of Italy. "One has to see it," he used to say when he came home; and he lamented the fact that Brother André had never seen it. Then he always ended by remembering in how fair a land Brother André had now found himself. "Better than Italy," he said to comfort himself.

Back of the little chapel there was still wild woodland. Brother André had been accustomed to look out hopefully, for he wanted to have a park there and statues that would depict scenes in the life of Saint Joseph. As yet that has not been done, for there is the basilica to finish first. And after all crypt and basilica are really statues to Saint Joseph, just as they are the prayer in stone of Brother André. In fact every single stone of the edifice is a witness, for a great many of them are ex-votos, bought with money left as an answer to the power of Saint Joseph. All together the stones that build the shrine are a realisation of promises given by the Faithful to Brother André. They had pledged themselves to build a monument worthy of Saint Joseph, who was the patron and benefactor of them all.

The little single stones, bought by the poor, and the great stones bought by those with more money to spend, all represent healings and conversions and hopes fulfilled. The bas-relief of the pediment is in Latin, but it says to each one who comes what Brother André said over and over in his own tongue : "*Ite ad Joseph.*" "Go to Joseph," he always bade his clients.

For all the people who come to the Oratory there is always one focal point other than the altar itself, and it has been so ever since the day in January when Brother André was buried. That is the niche, almost a lateral chapel, where Brother André lies and which the pilgrim seeks, once he has made his obeisance to Our Lord. It can be seen the moment one enters the great doors of the church for it is directly opposite them ; but one must first pass by Our Lord. That is as Brother André would have it : to adore Christ of the Eucharist before visiting His servant.

On the plain marble nothing has been added to the plain words : "Frère André." But the fresco which was blessed in 1940 now gives a setting for the casket. The central panel delicately coloured represents the death of Saint Joseph. He is sitting up, very worn and weary ; supporting him is Mary, and before him stands the young Christ. Back of the tomb itself, below the fresco, is the painting of the cross with the instruments of the Passion. On each side of the central picture is painted one of the two defenders and protectors of Brother André ; on the left, the saint whose name he bore—Andrew. On the right is his Guardian Angel.

Very near it is another shallow chapel filled to overflowing with great racks of glowing little lights. On either side are hung piles of crutches and pictures of children, or perhaps a flowered card with : "Thanks to Saint Joseph and Brother André" written on it. To some of the crutches are attached the certificates of physicians, witnessing the truth of the cures. There is always someone kneeling at the tomb, and usually there is more than one. Some are newcomers who know that the influence which built that great, stone church is still with them. Some are people who told the Brother their troubles in the past and are murmuring them to him now. And there are many who knew him in the past or were healed by him.

One day, a few years after Brother André's death, Polydore Beaulne who had been healed years ago and had worked for him afterwards, came to the tomb, his finger crushed so badly he could not work because it would not bend. He was sure Brother André would remember him. So he put the hurt finger on the granite of the tomb and said a prayer to Saint Joseph. Then he came closer and whispered: "Heal it for me, Brother—I need it so much to work with."

In the morning he was back again. "Brother, thank you for your help," he murmured in the chapel. Then he hailed a passing priest. "See, Father"; and he held up his finger and bent it without pain. "A little miracle, but it shows he does not forget us who loved him and had faith in him."

Mrs. Mivelle came to pay a visit to the grave to pray for her husband who had died the year before. It was in 1908 that Brother André had healed him whom physicians declared incurable and he had lived to be seventy-nine years old. Father Cornish, who established at the old man's request the Holy Hour in his church, came in 1941 to make a novena and went back feeling greatly improved in health.

One family came bearing a strange ex-voto offering to the shrine: the bandages and batting removed from a child's eye some twenty-six years before. Brother André had told them the doctors were wrong, that the child did not need to have an eye removed. "Keep the stuff on till you get home," he told them, "then take it off and rub the eye with the oil and a medal. He will get better." That had been twenty-six years before. The child—a husky man now—still had both his eyes.

Often a returning pilgrim told of a cure of years before. There was the woman who had met Brother André when he came on a visit to her home town. She had a badly ankylosed condition of the joints, and was hoping to present her petition, but was waiting until others had spoken to him. As she stood in a group of friends near him he suddenly looked toward her and smilingly said, "They say you are sick, but I don't believe it. You aren't sick. Just try to get down on your knees." With no hesitation she tried it and the condition had disappeared. Now, like others, she had come back to pray at his tomb.

Among visitors was a doctor who had been badly crippled, and he was painfully training himself to walk with crutches. But Brother André said to him, "You are a doctor. Have confidence. Saint Joseph will not let you lose so fair a future after so many sacrifices on the part of your parents. Try now to walk alone." At the second attempt he found he could do so ; "and the crutches have been here at the Oratory ever since," he said.

The cures were continuing, too. Brother André was still at work. During March of 1941, there had been as usual a novena to Saint Joseph. In the crowd was one old man who had been for thirty years dragging along on a crutch. He got around with great difficulty but he managed to come to the crypt morning and evening during the novena, and each day received Holy Communion.

After the Pontifical Mass on March 10th, there was suddenly a great stir and commotion in one part of the church. "A cure! A miracle!" ran the excited murmur. When one of the priests went to investigate he did not at first recognise the erect figure they were looking at as anyone he knew. Yet he did look familiar. It was not until next day he knew it was the pathetic cripple of the entire novena.

"Yes, I'm the man," he answered his questioner with a broad smile.

"And your crutch?"

"I left it at home this morning. All I need is a little cane and that is really not necessary," said the overjoyed man.

"Are you really sure that you can walk without crutches?"

"Sure, I can," and he proceeded to walk. It was the first day in thirty-two years that he had done so.

There are often interesting figures among those who come to give thanks for a favour received while away from the shrine. One day Father Brassard noticed during one of the Sunday torchlight processions for peace which were taking place frequently during the summer of 1941, a naval officer in the procession. He was struck by his devout attitude. Later he met him—an Englishman, Sir Robert Hornell, a convert since the last war, who came when he could to the shrine to ask Saint Joseph's protection for a voyage, and to get pictures of Brother André to give to his men. This time he was there to give thanks for a safe return.

"After the last war," said Admiral Hornell, "it was faith in God and the quiet assurance He was still with them—some of the French whose homes were only ruins in a devastated land. That showed me another world—and I became a Catholic. And I come here when I can for I feel that in Brother André and his marvellous living work lies the tie with the dear departed and with the Sacred Heart."

There are stories of conversions taking place on the stairs leading to the crypt—stairs of commonplace wood built into the stiff ascent of the mountain which are crowded with kneeling pilgrims every day. They stop at each step to pray, and strangers have been known to ask if this is a *Scala Sancta* which must be climbed in this way.

No, they are told, it is a spontaneous devotion that these men and women offer. There is a story of one young woman of the world whom a devout friend brought to the Oratory under pretext of showing her the countryside from the top of the mountain, but with the secret hope that the shrine might some day lead to her friend's conversion. At the foot of the stairs, the friend excused herself and asked her permission to wait while she joined the pilgrims climbing on their knees. She had, she explained, a great favour to ask. Some time later she was surprised to see this young woman of the world falling on her knees beside her. "I understood suddenly as I waited for you, what the great favour you are asking for is. It is my conversion." Before the year was out the worldly young lady was rapping on the door of Carmel and consecrating herself wholly to God.

In the meantime Saint Joseph was busily working on his roof. In 1939 the engineers had warned the Guardians of the Shrine that if the cement cover on the dome were exposed to the winter snow and ice it would likely be damaged. But expenses had been so heavy, it was impossible to permit this construction; so the risk had to be taken, covering up as much of the cement as possible and leaving the rest to Saint Joseph. A campaign was begun to cover the dome the following summer. This campaign was so successful, there was enough extra money left over, after the necessary work on the dome was finished, to place the granite at its base immediately. On Brother André's birthday of that year it was decided to bless the first stone which would then be hoisted to position as a symbol of the many that would soon follow.

On this occasion the Auxiliary Archbishop of Montreal officiated and Father Deguire gave an address of welcome. Father Cousineau, Superior General, came from Notre Dame to give an instruction each night of the novena. He had a very personal interest in it all, for he had been for three years rector of the shrine and had done much to aid in finishing the walls and erecting the dome. After the ceremonies were over and the stone safely in position, everyone agreed that Brother André could not have had a lovelier birthday gift than this.

CHAPTER TWELVE

HE WORKS IN HEAVEN AS ON EARTH

THE great edifice which he had entered daily for so many years was really never anything but a means to an end for Brother André. It would not have mattered to him how great the building, had there not been at the same time a temple built, as Saint Teresa used to phrase it, in the heart of each man and woman who came there.

To him the shrine was always a means to an end and never the end itself. The small primitive chapel was a means, and so was the great basilica. The one difference in value in the two edifices in Brother André's eyes was that the basilica would bring more souls to God because it could house a much larger number of people. To him the greatest, in fact the only thing in the world of value, was faith; and he had a serene belief that it was the greatest armour with which to be girded—the armour with which the mightiest enemies against God and men would be routed.

His work had its beginning with the beginning of the great evil of our time—the poisoning of the world with lies and hatred against Christianity. And he knew that only love and faith could drive these from the hearts of men.

He had sometimes felt very unhappy about conditions and about people too. "Miracles are performed," he sighed one day, "so that the world may open its eyes and be converted, but it seems as if it were blind." Yet he never despaired. His heart was too full of the joy of God for that. "Don't ever be sad," he used to tell his friends. "Be gay. Remember the advice of Saint Teresa of Avila, who did not like scowling saints and who used to say, 'My daughters, do not be stupid creatures supernaturally when we are such by nature'."

His good humour was nearly always a visible thing. Only if curiosity brought a man or woman to the shrine and not faith, or only if the power for the cures was attributed to him did he become sad or displeased. When one visitor said bluntly, "You are always putting great value on Saint Joseph; we obtain all sorts of favours from you and the saint remains deaf to our pleas," he was so upset at such an utter lack of understanding that he was taken with a chill and had to be kept in bed for several days. But he learned to bear that cross, as he did too that of loneliness, than which there is perhaps none harder. For all his great following he was often misunderstood, libelled and calumniated when he was not at fault.

One day he showed great annoyance when a visitor came to him and asked, whether ingenuously or on purpose, "Will you tell me by what magic you work your cures?" But these were really the exceptions; the great majority who came to him knew that his work was on a high supernatural plane and that the cures were not his; that he was merely an agent for Saint Joseph and that back of Saint Joseph was God.

In the summer of 1936 two cures had been announced in one afternoon, both remarkable and both sudden. One was a sick man who had been carried in and, later, walked out. The other was a paralytic who was brought in by a friend who shook his head at the folly of bringing him at all, and continued shaking his head even in Brother André's office. "If he cures him that will be something," he said doubtfully to the man beside him. When this second cure occurred a Protestant who was standing watching him was heard to say under his breath, "God is great." That statement when told to Brother André made him smile with happiness for he knew that man had truly understood.

Later in the afternoon Father Clement began to tease him, while the Brother was reading quietly as if nothing unusual had happened. "I hear two people went into your office today in a bad humour."

Brother André, well aware he was referring to the two sensational cures, unsmilingly said, "You know very well that was not my fault. You must blame the good God for that." When the paralytic tried to convey to him his deep thanks, Brother André had said simply, "Saint Joseph decided you need the use of your two feet. Thank him."

He never got over his surprise that he had actually been allowed to become a religious. What service could God have reserved for him to render to the Community at whose door he had come knocking? And he often laughed to Father Clement at the joke that God was playing on Himself. But Father Clement thought that God, who is so partial to humble souls, no doubt loved to see them carry out a giant's work.

Archbishop Bruchési, who had come to know him well through the years, said that his candour and his humble simplicity always struck him each time he met him. That was a very true estimate, for Brother André always spoke of Saint Joseph and the Holy Family with the natural simplicity of someone who speaks affectionately of a well-known relative; and when he prayed aloud to his patron it sounded as if he were really conversing with him.

Our Lord told the people of His time to become as little children if they wished to enter Heaven. Brother André was always a child at heart. He had always kept his simple faith and love and remained forever young. In default of knowing the world he knew God.

The Patron of workmen was the proper saint for him to cherish. For the life of Saint Joseph was a hidden one. His choice was humility. And Brother André's life was an imitation

of the life of his great patron. To remain in the shadow so
that God would be glorified in the light—that was the life of
Brother André, and his life was like that of Saint Joseph. It
was a triumph of humility over all worldly things. He lived
his entire life with and for God.

His devotion, beyond all the others, was to the Passion, just
as the greatest celebrations at the Oratory are celebrations
commemorating the Eucharist. As he repeated over and over,
the temporary favours granted there, are, as they have always
been, for the purpose of opening the eyes of people to God.
The chief value and the glory of Brother André's Oratory is
that there one breathes in the supernatural, and receives grace,
a gift that comes from faith. It is a place where all may obtain
spiritual strength which is greater and more lasting than any
physical favour.

For those who come to the Oratory must leave the world
behind when they enter there, to hear its clamour grow fainter
and then disappear as they hear instead new sounds that emerge.
Sometimes these sounds are audible to the human ear—sounds
of prayer and singing; but often they are heard only by the
spirit. Then is wrought a great miracle of spiritual healing.

Faith that was weak and wavering receives in the church on
Mount Royal aid from the reservoirs of strength stored there;
and consciences dulled for years became quickened, until the
pilgrims look about for the confessional in the shadows of the
great crypt. Long after the ceremonies are over these pilgrims
linger in the pews; and one feels sure that, after the collective
prayers heard earlier from the priests at the altar, now over
the entire building, are rising to God the individual prayers
that become one great voice of unspoken reverence and
thanksgiving.

It was really the Protestants who gave to Brother André the
name of Miracle Man, a facile phrase which Brother André

himself did not like, but which has a value. Catholics were more likely to call him a saint, and there is no doubt, had he heard his devoted clients call him such, he would have been both angry and puzzled. But after his death more than one bishop called him "a true saint," and many letters from the clergy expressed a hope that the lay Brother of Mount Royal would soon be canonized.

To understand his true importance in the world of the spirit that centres always about a church, one must have been at Mount Royal during the days that followed his death, must have watched the thousands who were storming the basilica to see him once more, to touch his hand or his garments. And one must have a record of the many conversions that occurred after his burial. The priests who were there during those days could tell of these conversions and of the many visitors who returned to the practice of their faith during that week. The thousands of letters that told of favours received were witnesses too of how many bodies and souls had been healed by the influence of the chapel and the crypt.

In the beginning of his work he said to a friend, "Oh, if I only had a priest to care for all the souls of the people who come to see me. They are well disposed when they go from me—but will they go to confession after they leave me?" He had his answer long ago. He had his priests, in ever increasing numbers, to set their seal on the work he had begun.

Thousands who come to the Oratory ask the same insistent question, "When will Brother André be canonized?" And among religious of all ranks the story of Father Frederic, a Franciscan whose cause has been lately introduced at Rome, is very typical. He came to the Oratory one day for a visit. "I have come to ask Brother André," he said, "what is required to become such a saint as he is."

The rector took him to the little chapel and they climbed

the stairs to Brother André's attic room. When he heard the
approach of visitors he came out to greet them. But when
Father Frederic fell on his knees and said, "Bless me, Brother
André," the lay Brother was thrown into evident confusion.
He lifted the priest up hastily and sank instead to his own
knees. "Oh, no, Father, it is you who must bless me," he
insisted.

Those who hope for canonization are happy that the pre-
liminary process is begun. In October, 1940, the rector of the
shrine, Father Deguire, received from the Superior General of
the Congregation of Holy Cross a letter naming him procurator
in the beatification and canonization of Brother André; also
he authorised him to select assistants for the work, and to
collect as well as to administer the money necessary for the
cause.

In November of that year the newly appointed procurator
wrote to the Archbishop of Montreal for authority to begin
inquiry into the writings of Brother André, and to consider
the entire subject of his reputed sanctity, his virtues and the
authenticity of his miracles.

The archbishop wrote that it was with joy and confidence he
gave permission; and in his letter expressed his own feelings:
"Remembering his exalted life and witnessing his amazing work
and its benefits, are we not justified in expecting the Church
to glorify on earth this worthy servant of God, this great
apostle of devotion to Saint Joseph?" He also appointed a
tribunal for the investigation.

Early in 1942 the little room in the college, where Brother
André had so long been porter, was restored. It had been
demolished in 1931 because the extra space was needed badly,
but for some time its reconstruction had been suggested and
planned; Then, as part of the celebration of Montreal's third
centenary, it was rebuilt. The three wall sections and the door

are back now in their original places. The old couch, flat and hard, is there; and so is the picture of Saint Joseph which Brother André had set up for remembrance; also the desk, and the crucifix. To those who remember an earlier time, it would seem Brother André might come walking in again any moment, back from a visit to the sick in the village or from prayers in the chapel.

About this time, too, the ceremony for the blessing of the sick was first expressed in English, and crowds of English-speaking pilgrims took part. At one such ceremony Father Cornish of Keeseville carried the monstrance to the communion rail where hundreds of sick, some of them carried there, awaited the blessing of their Lord.

Meanwhile, in the great crypt which his patient prayers and work have raised, Brother André lies and still receives his visitors. There are many physical healings reported. There are even more numerous healings of the soul. Over the black granite of his tomb are heaped letters containing requests and hopes and thanks. Canada and the United States and South America and France and Ireland and other lands send petitions —testimony to the power of Brother André's intercession.

Long ago he said, "When someone does something good on earth it is nothing compared to what he will be able to do once he gets to Heaven." And the crowds and the letters show Brother André is keeping his word. That remark was made in the same spirit of another assertion attributed to him later. "The thing that consoles me is that after every great ordeal, the Oratory expands and grows so."

Once it was a solitude on a mountain. Now from early dawn to night one hears the sound of voices and of carriages and cars and the movements of feet going up the grey old steps. In good weather in the summer and fall there are five thousand at the morning Masses and at evening Benediction, and special feast days bring as many as twenty-five or fifty thousand visitors. They come to the shrine happy or sad, troubled in soul or body, rich or poor, but one and all they leave richer in spirit, with greater hope and renewed courage to meet the world beyond the basilica.

When they come to the city as when they leave it they see at first glance and at last, the mighty shrine that seems to tower into the clouds in day time ; and when it is night they see the golden glow of the great cross high on the dome of the basilica.

No human action alone could ever explain this mighty structure. Yet for all its grandeur, it is the result of the millions of small donations given by the humble and the poor, as Brother André was humble and poor, as Saint Joseph was humble and poor and as Our Lord was poor during all His earthly life.

It is the prayer of a lay Brother carved in stone and the work of the many who loved him, and of the Cross they all served. It never has had any publicity plan for its work, nor any staggering advertising campaign, nor any appeals for aid other than those projected in the *Annals*. It has grown rather as did the old-world cathedrals, although its present proportions achieved in less than forty years express something of a miracle. There were many more timid souls somewhat aghast at the daring of the builders, but perhaps in that the Oratory is rather like the cathedral at Seville in Spain. There, hundreds of years ago, when the authorities of the diocese held a meeting to devise how best to combat the effect of the lovely Moorish cathedral in their city, one man said, "Let us build so that future generations will call us visionaries."

"But wait," said Monsignor Bruchési, "until the basilica is blessed. Then we shall see the crowds." Then he stood looking down at an open air Mass where thousands were massed everywhere ; on the steps, on the roads, almost in the street itself.

That will be a wonderful day. But even now there is a blessing over everything at the shrine. It rains and snows sometimes up there on the mountain, but the pilgrims all agree that no matter what the weather, all the days at the shrine are beautiful days.

The shrine is built on all the Gospels and on all the Parables. For these were all the teaching, all the practices of Brother André. "Everything reminds us of the Cross, as we ourselves are made in the form of a cross." And so it was with Brother André. Love for him meant the Cross ; and the shrine at Mount Royal is the result of that love. It is the exemplified Calvary of which he never ceased dreaming. The shrine was built out of that dreaming.

Friend of the people, of the humble and obscure, of the sick in body and soul, reader of hearts, sympathetic always with those who were hard working and weary, as his Master had been—this was the life of Brother André. "It does not matter," he said one day to Father Clement, "what happens to me if only the people do not suffer."

And the great building with its towering cross, its artistry of line and form, its lovely windows, its beautifully carved statues, and the awkward little chapel with its old-fashioned pictures, its crude altar, say the same thing to the pilgrims who come there. For all day long and all night long it seems to them as if Brother André were calling to a tired, suffering, bewildered world the words of his Master: "Come to Me, all you that labour and are burdened, and I will refresh you."